The Circle of Memory

Also by SUBHASH KAK

The Architecture of Knowledge
The Nature of Physical Reality
The Astronomical Code of the Ṛgveda
The Gods Within
Computation in Ancient India
Matter and Mind: The Vaiśeṣika Sūtra of Kaṇāda
Mind and Self: Patañjali's Yoga Sūtra and Modern Science
The Prajñā Sūtra: Aphorisms of Intuition
The Wishing Tree
In Search of the Cradle of Civilization
The Aśvamedha
Arrival and Exile
The Loom of Time

The Circle of Memory
An Autobiography

Subhash Kak

Mount Meru Publishing

Library and Archives Canada Cataloguing in Publication

Kak, Subhash, 1947-, author

The circle of memory: an autobiography/SubhashKak.

Issued in print and electronic formats.

ISBN 978-1-988207-17-9 (softcover).--ISBN 978-1-988207-18-6(HTML)

1. Kak, Subhash, 1947-. 2. Computer scientist--Oklahoma--Biography. I. Title.

| QA76.2.K35A3 2016 | 621.39092 | C2016-907618-0 |
| | | C2016-907619-9 |

The views expressed in this book belong solely to the author and do not necessarily reflect the views of the publisher. Neither the author nor publisher is liable for any loss or damages resulting from the use of information presented in this book. Neither the author nor publisher makes any representation or warranty with respect to the accuracy or completeness of the information presented in this book.

Published in 2016 by:
Mount Meru publishing
P.O. Box 30026
Cityside Postal Outlet PO
Mississauga, Ontario
Canada   L4Z 0B6
Email: mountmerupublishing@gmail.com

ISBN 978-1-988207-17-9

Cover image: Pixabay (https://pixabay.com)

CONTENTS

PREFACE

Although this is principally the story of my life as a scientist, it is also about the winds of change — some good, and some bad — that swept the world this past half century. Technology has changed the way we experience the world, and pervasive automation is leading to a permanent loss of jobs. In politics, communism as an idea may be dead, but neoliberal dispensation has not brought peace and prosperity. Unprecedented migration of people across the globe has created new problems of reconciliation of cultures, and science is nowhere near explaining the problem of consciousness.

When I was a child in Kashmir, our lives were simple, perhaps like that of our forebears centuries ago, mostly without modern conveniences such as electricity, telephone, or running water. The recent political independence of India seemed a big thing, a major break with history, and there was hope that the future will be shining. But independence brought to the surface a religious conflict that had remained frozen for couple of centuries, and this conflict has now travelled to Europe, Africa, and Asia.

I wished to be a writer and a scientist and I was advised that the engineering degree was a good starting point. The leap from a childhood of books and few machines to one where I had to design advanced computing systems turned out to be a short one. I spent nearly a decade teaching at IIT but then moved west to be part of the larger community of scientists.

My research program became progressively broader and, in time, it got to include ancient history and art. From there to contentious debates in the halls of universities and speeches in public places turned out to be a short journey.

Along the way I became aware of the different ways of the sciences and the humanities. Mathematical and physical arguments are easier to check for basic errors than those in the social sciences and history. You may not divide by zero, because if you did then you could show, for example, that $2 = 3$ (because $2/0 = 3/0$); likewise, any system that delivers more work than the energy it takes in is a logically impossible perpetual motion machine.

In the social sciences authors sometimes get carried away by ideas that are unfalsifiable or logically inconsistent and since these ideas are repeated in the echo chambers of the academia, it can take a generation or two, or even longer, to realize this.

I speak in this book principally of my intellectual journey and not specific events as they unfolded, although there is some of that as well.

It is difficult to write about the past. Time may lend perspective, but for those who have traveled beyond unquestioned belief, the past is less than living history. Life's insights do not emerge out of a few dramatic, central experiences but by the slow influence of hundreds of seemingly insignificant events. The way we looked at reality when we were young is different from how it appears now. With each stage in the sequence of life-transitions, we shed parts of the previous self.

Subhash Kak
Stillwater, Oklahoma
Diwali, October 30, 2016

1. A TIME OF GIFTS

Ours is a gilded age. Machines do our bidding, choicest foods from faraway lands are served at the table, and we remain connected to others on the globe through smart phones. But with plenty has come despair and a pall has descended that some are trying to forget with drugs and alcohol. As the story of the churning of the ocean informs, the elixir of immortality comes together with the most destructive poison.

As a child in Kashmir, things couldn't be more different. We huddled around a weak kerosene lamp to do homework at night. The fear of war was always in the back of our minds. Pakistan sent tribal proxies into Kashmir in the late forties, wreaking havoc, and there was apprehension that this will be repeated, as was to happen in 1965, and then many more times a quarter century later. As children we worried about the religious roots of the Pakistani hatred towards India. We wondered if India had become a pawn in the rivalry between the West and the Communists and if the jihadi wars of the medieval period were to visit us again.

Our lives were changing and by the time I was in high school plumbing and electricity had arrived. India was beggared by the British Raj and much needed to be done to develop basic infrastructure for which engineers were needed. This is how my brother, Avinash, and I became engineers. From there doing Ph.D. at IIT Delhi seemed the natural next step. Avinash received a teaching offer at Purdue University in the US even before he had finished writing his thesis; I decided to stay on after IIT Delhi offered me a faculty position.

In the beginning of my studies, after the initial couple of meeting with my supervisor, P.V. Indiresan, who was also the department head, I was granted freedom to work as I pleased with the expectation that I shall report progress once or so a year. Soon before the end of the minimum requirement of three years of studentship, I presented Dr Indiresan a bound thesis. He gave assent and my thesis was sent to two external examiners, one in the US and another at IIT Kanpur. I was twenty-three and had my Ph.D., but the interesting part of my research was yet to come.

The excitement of the faculty position wore off rather quickly. I was dissatisfied because most of my colleagues were content with their classroom work, whereas my ambition was in research and writing. During my Ph.D., I published results in signal theory, which is fundamental to computer science, and now I began studying quantum theory to examine the question of information at a deeper level.

Knowing of my unhappiness, IIT mollified me by appointing me assistant professor (equivalent to associate professor in the US) in three years. Then, in 1975, I went to Imperial College London on a British Council fellowship at the end of which I spent a summer at Bell Laboratories in Murray Hill in New Jersey.

Having rubbed shoulders with the world's best at Bell Labs, I became even more dissatisfied with the academic environment at IIT. Next year, in 1977, I was offered an endowed visiting professorship by Technion but the administration refused to grant me leave. Two years later I resigned and accepted a professorship at Louisiana State University in the United States.

During my student years, it was not science or engineering or business that was in the news. Radio and newspapers served as the voice of the government, and the idea of socialism pushed all others aside. The champions of socialist change wanted to create a new India that was not burdened by history. They imagined they were revolutionaries in having chosen their way of self-reliance, independent of both the West and the Soviets. They believed that the poverty of India was more a consequence of its social institutions than colonial history or lack of an educated workforce.

Socialism was a nationalistic response to the prevailing view that Indian history was a continuing domination by invaders starting with the Aryans from the northwest around 3,500 years ago to the English who came more recently. The new political masters of India wished to forestall any future control by outsiders by centralization of executive power, industrial activity, and education.

In reality, Indian history is a complicated story in which there were incursions from outside but also expansion of Indian merchants beyond the seas to Southeast Asia, and influence of Indian businessmen and missionaries in Eurasia and Africa. The idea of Aryan invasions around 1500 BCE was a theory that went against literary evidence but it was embraced by colonial historians as justification for the Raj, and once established in the academy it exercised powerful influence on the Westernized Indian elite. In time it found backing by historians in Europe who added antiquity to their culture and civilization by claiming that the Vedas were authored by Europeans who migrated to India.

Many scholars had long argued against the idea of invasions, but they were ignored. Then in 1987 the British archaeologist Colin Renfrew's book *Archaeology and Language* synthesized the latest evidence to arrive at a new

3

model that saw the spread of Aryans through agriculture at a much earlier period of 7500 BCE. Seeing the importance of this book in restarting the debate on Indian history, I reviewed it in the Times of India.

Sita Ram Goel, a leading independent-minded thinker and publisher of books under the imprint Voice of India, told me later that this review marked the turning point in nationalist circles. The ideas in the book were a challenge to the Aryan invasion theory on which Indian polity was built. If the foundation was hollow then a new authentic structure could be built in its place.

My work on ancient Indian science, showing its continuity with the historical period, was to contribute to the new synthesis. *In Search of the Cradle of Civilization*, which I co-wrote with well-known scholars Georg Feuerstein and David Frawley, was the first book to challenge the invasion theory.

How I got to know Frawley is an interesting story. On a family trip by van from Louisiana to the national parks in the West, we came across a flyer about a Hanuman temple in the town of Taos in New Mexico. Curious, we visited the temple the next day and found that it had been established by the American devotees of the famous saint Neem Karoli Baba. There one of the devotees told me about David Frawley's work on the Veda and soon we got in touch. At that time we did not know that Kainchi Dham, Neem Karoli Baba's ashram in the Himalayas, was well known in technology circles and Steve Jobs and other tech titans had spent time there.

———

Initially my technical research at IIT was in the mainstream field of mathematical information theory. In the past seventy years, this subject has guided the development of signal processing and other applied areas of computing and entertainment that have transformed modern life.

As it was being realized that society will increasingly use digital technologies, I moved on to the problem of cryptography. At Bell Laboratories, my collaborator N.S. Jayant and I developed one of the very first methods of speech encryption. Later, I took up the problem of secure communication between many parties where one must find methods to authenticate users who are at remote locations. In time parts of this research became embedded in the technology that created the electronic commerce revolution.

———

Meanwhile, while exploring the history of computing algorithms, I stumbled onto Pāṇini. His grammar of Sanskrit has been hailed by scholars as an astonishing feat, with the famous American linguist Leonard Bloomfield calling it "one of the greatest monuments of human intelligence." Amazingly, it used to be believed that there was no science, or even knowledge of writing, in India during Pāṇini's time. Since I don't believe that science emerges without appropriate context, I decided to investigate the original sources. As I examined these texts, layer by layer, I discovered a long-lost astronomy of the Vedas with implications for chronology. This discovery contradicted the prevailing belief that Indian sciences were derived from Mesopotamia and it offered a new understanding of Indian culture by showing that Vedic ritual had a scientific basis.

The new findings are consistent with the traditional belief that the Vedas address both the knowledge of outer reality and the subjective self. Elements of Indian culture code this knowledge but this encoding is mostly forgotten. The discovery of this code hidden in the deepest layers of

Vedic ritual had shone new light on many aspects of Indian culture.

I wrote for scholarly journals in India and the West on these matters. Several books such as *The Astronomical Code of the Ṛgveda, The Gods Within, The Wishing Tree,* and *The Aśvamedha* presented the new understanding. The work was received favorably by most in academic and lay circles. Literally every week, I was invited to universities and community functions to speak on these findings. I also addressed public meetings, temples and churches, was interviewed on radio and television, and traveled many times overseas to lecture in India and Europe. The Public Television Network in Holland recreated the Vedic altar ritual for a documentary.

I also wrote on various subjects of history of science for the 100-volume History of Science, Philosophy and Culture in Indian Civilization at the invitation of its editor, the scholarly Govind Chandra Pande, which made this work accessible to readers in India. Pande was also a poet and when he found that I had written books of poetry in English, he arranged to get my collection of Hindi poems published. Somewhat later the chief editor of the series, Debi Prasad Chattopadhyaya, asked me to write a book presenting an overview of physics, neuroscience, and consciousness which I did under the title *The Architecture of Knowledge.*

An interesting implication of my Vedic research concerned the Mitanni kings of West Asia of second millennium BCE. If Vedic astronomy was older than this period, as is suggested by my research, then the Mitannis, who worshiped Vedic deities, had an Indian connection. The Mitannis could not be an advance guard of the Indo-European migrations to India for they were a ruling minority and the language they used was Indo-Aryan and not Indo-Iranian. The Mitannis ruled before the rise of the Abrahamic religions, so one could speculate that through them India had influenced the very beginnings of these religions.

My analysis of the Veda was more than an esoteric exercise. The Vedas claim to be the science of consciousness (*ātma vidyā*), which is a topic of immense interest to contemporary physicists and neuroscientists, and the understanding of ritual is central to anthropology. So if there was anything to these claims, one could expect that the Veda derived traditions will receive greater attention in the future.

During the years that followed, I was able to enlarge upon the initial insights. I studied temple architecture and was invited to formulate a theory of music by the composer Jose Maceda that led eventually to a documentary movie on Hindustani classical music. The work on archaeoastronomy, which is the astronomy related to the orientations of ancient buildings and monuments, led me to examine other ancient civilizations such as the Inca. In particular, I studied an old computation board that suggested hitherto unknown aspects of Inca astronomy.

Back in Kashmir, a tragedy was unfolding. Jihadi militants, some inspired by religious zeal and others who were proxies for Pakistan, began a campaign of terror against Hindus in the late 1980s. It began with random killings, with mobs burning down temples and properties. There were political demonstrations against the government and calls for an end to the rule of the kafirs or Indians. The atmosphere was highly charged in the autumn of 1989.

In January 1990, newspapers began to publish menacing articles. The campaign reached a crescendo on January 19 when loudspeakers from mosques asked Hindus to convert, leave, or be killed. Posters on the walls of public buildings tried to soften the blow by saying that only men

7

may leave and women could stay, anticipating the horrors that were to befall Yazidi women in Iraq twenty-five years later.

The rule of law had broken down and the government was unable to guarantee security. People had no choice but leave. Literally the entire valley was emptied of its Hindu population, with people fleeing by truck, bus or any other transport. These refugees didn't just lose their homes and property, they also lost their dignity. They were housed in makeshift camps in Jammu City and other places in India and many still languish there, nearly three decades after the exodus.

The diasporic Kashmiri community in the United States decided to bring this tragedy before the larger public. Several of us went around the country speaking at public meetings on what had happened, hoping that politicians and the media will take note and the government would pressure the puppeteers in Pakistan to change their policy. It was a very emotional tour as we heard first hand stories of the horrors from refugees who had managed to arrive in the US.

Bill Clinton's administration had a close relationship with Pakistan at that time and so nothing happened. The terrorists went on with their killings.

My parents had left Kashmir and settled down in Delhi a few years earlier but other relatives in Kashmir had to abandon their homes. More than individual loss, this exile was the end of the story of a centuries-old extraordinary culture devoted to excellence in literature, philosophy, and the arts. Even though similar violence had occurred nearly once every century since the onset of Islamic Rule in the fourteenth century, this was the first complete expulsion of the people connected to Kashmir's ancient history and culture. We didn't know that this was a foretelling of similar tragedies to come elsewhere.

The historian Stanley Wolpert invited me to UCLA in April 2002 for a conference on Kashmir. It was organized by the UCLA Burkle Center for International Relations with the title "Kashmir: Ways to Help Resolve One of the World's Most Dangerous Conflicts." New York had been attacked the previous year and influential people in Pakistan were speaking of the use of nuclear weapons to seize Kashmir. American policy makers were worried about things going out of hand and they had the Burkle Center put together a panel of speakers with different points of view to open lines of communication.

The participants assembled in the evening for a social at the Wolpert home. He and his wife, Dorothy, were most gracious hosts. I was shocked however by the arguments advanced by Pakistani military officers. They were polite and spoke in clipped accent but their fanaticism was appalling.

The next day at the meeting, after a general overview by Wolpert, I presented the perspective of Kashmiri refugees. There was a spokesman for the Pakistani viewpoint, and the historian Damodar SarDesai of UCLA presented the Indian perspective. Sadly, the conversations at the meeting were not continued later, as the organizers had hoped.

Soon after this, Wolpert was appointed chief editor of a new Encyclopedia of India to be published by Charles Scribner's Sons of New York. He wrote giving me free rein to pick topics and I ended up writing on eighteen different topics, ranging from Kashmir to Āyurveda, that turned out to be just one less than the number he wrote himself.

———

The focus of my technical research had meanwhile switched to the foundations of cognitive science (especially neural networks) and quantum information theory.

The field of neural networks became very important in the eighties as cognitive scientists began investigating brain behavior. It is not possible to analyze this behavior by exhaustive analysis, as the number of neurons in the brain is astronomically large, nearly equal to the number of stars in the universe. Operationally, each neuron is a simple system, that either fires (that is, sends out electrical pulses) or remains quiescent although the degree of connectivity between different neurons varies.

In 1949, the Canadian psychologist Donald Hebb suggested that learned behavior and memories were coded in the connection strengths between neurons. He proposed that if two neurons fire then the synapses between them get strengthened and vice versa, and this is continued until such time that the stimulus maps into a resonance associated with the network.

Now scientists wished to examine general properties of networks of computing elements in the hope that these will reveal how memories are stored and images and sounds recognized. A method, named later as the backpropagation algorithm, was soon discovered which allowed the determination of the connection strengths for a multi-stage network of neurons that mapped input data to different classes. Somewhat later I discovered a much simpler method of finding these connection strengths instantaneously.

There was much excitement around the world about building neural network-based machines for artificial intelligence (AI) applications. But it was clear that the path to the computer emulation of the mind was far off. Much about the workings of the brain remains unknown. How are memories stored? What are the mechanisms behind short-term and long-term memories? How is the pattern at the far end of the vision system recognized? Where does the recognizer sit?

It was soon realized that these networks could not address the question of the nature of awareness, which cannot be a property of a single neuron with just two states. If awareness is distributed activity over many neurons, how is such activity recognized? Some argued that the complexity of connections causes the emergence of awareness; others suggested that it is a consequence of quantum processing in the brain.

Quantum theory is the deepest theory of physics we have. In the classical world objects have well-defined properties, whereas in the quantum world one cannot speak of such properties prior to measurement. A quantum state is a superposition of mutually exclusive attributes, such as up and down spins at the same time, and a quantum particle can be at more than one place simultaneously. In one interpretation of quantum theory, it is the measurement by the observer that causes the many possibilities to collapse to a specific one, which brings us back to the question of awareness.

I examined the possible application of quantum theory to biology, proposing that the structure of the biological system itself is in a state of superposition of many metastable states. These states form a spectrum, and I gave such brain processing the name *quantum neural computing*.

I suggested further that brain behavior is associated with three languages that may be called associative, reorganizational, and quantum. The associative language is the ordinary language of communication that is mediated by neurotransmitters and electrical impulses; the reorganizational language is one in which the subsystems reorganize and in doing so change the modes of communication; and the quantum language is characterized by superpositions.

11

But what about creativity? If ordinary behavior is determined by prior causes, perhaps this is not so when we are creative for then we seem to have access to unexplainable insight. Certain kind of creativity could have been hard-wired into the brain by evolution, but this does not explain anomalous quantitative knowledge, the most dramatic example of which is the speed of light mentioned in a fourteenth century commentary by Sāyaṇa.

A more recent example of anomalous creativity is the work of the great mathematician Srinivasa Ramanujan, who died in 1920 at the age of 32. His notebook, which was lost and forgotten for about 50 years and published only in 1988, contains several thousand formulas -- without proof, in different areas of mathematics -- that were well ahead of their time, and the methods by which he found the formulas remain elusive. Ramanujan himself claimed that the formulas were revealed to him in his sleep. Is it possible that the creative process draws upon the unconscious in a manner that cannot be explained in rational terms?

Quantum theory shows that properties of objects that are far apart can remain entangled. One of the puzzles is why these entanglements are not ordinarily experienced. I believe *the principle of veiled nonlocality* hides the nonlocal entanglements that exist in our world of which, in our personal lives, we are intuitively convinced. Our theories are an attempt to present our experience of the world in a local sense, in accord with the nature of our cognitions, and this appears to be similar to the working of māyā.

2. The Vale of Kashmir

I grew up surrounded by the extraordinary beauty of Kashmir and soon learnt bits and pieces of its history from stories told by relatives. During holidays, we picnicked in the lovely public gardens with water-fountains and terraces that are part of Kashmir's recent history. I also became aware of things that pointed to an old world that had passed. These were ruins of centuries-old magnificent stone temples with elegance of proportion, symmetry and balance.

We saw the waterlines along the high karewas (tableland, *wudar* in Kashmiri) that made it clear that once upon a time, a long time ago, the entire valley was under water. Legends told us that this lake, called Satīsar, was eventually drained making the place inhabitable.

Kashmir's geographical location partly explains its cultural history. Its natural beauty and temperate climate may be the reason that Kashmiris have a strong tradition in the arts. Ancient geographers saw Kashmir as the stamen of the flower at the centre of Asia, from the corners of which emanated the four petals of Iran, Turan, Tibet, and the Punjab. Kashmir's location in this scheme was recognition that it was a meeting ground for trade and ideas for these four regions. It was to become more than a meeting ground; it was the land where an attempt was made to reconcile opposites by analysis and bold conception.

Kashmir's nearness to rich trade routes brought it considerable wealth. Kashmiris became interpreters of the

Indian civilization, authoring many fundamental synthesizing and expository works.

The Kārkoṭa dynasty of the seventh and eighth centuries provides us with the first authentic accounts of the government in the Vale. Lalitāditya (724-60) was the outstanding king of this dynasty who built the famed Sun temple of Mārtaṇḍa. In the 9th century, Avantivarman built a grand capital south of Srinagar whose ruins can still be seen.

The geography of the valley comes with cycles of flood and famine. In the 19th century, Walter Lawrence estimated that the famine of 1831 reduced the population of the valley from 800,000 to 200,000; another famine of 1878 took the lives of three-fifths of the population.

The history of Islam in Kashmir goes back to 1339 when the throne, weakened by decades of internal strife and external pressure from the north after the fall of Khotan in 1006, was seized by a Swati immigrant, Shah Mir, who deposed Queen Koṭa Rani, the daughter of a previous king. Shah Mir's descendants ruled until mid-sixteenth century when it became a part of the Mughal Empire during Akbar's reign.

Religious identity became sharp during the reign of Qutb-ud-din (1373-89) with Muslims from west and central Asia coming to the valley for refuge. Sikandar Butshikan (1389-1413) destroyed temples and images, forcibly converted Hindus to Islam and expelled others. Sikandar's son Zain-ul-Abidin (1420-70) was liberal, and many Hindus who had fled during his father's reign returned to the valley. Later history had periods of good government interspersed with harsh persecution as during the proselytization by Shams-ud-din Iraqi in 1492.

Those who left the valley during the Mughal times remember their origins well and have held on to old customs. The social fabric of the community, which is called the birādari, facilitates this memory. In 1752, Kashmir was annexed by Afghanistan and ruled badly. After the violent cleansing of the 1990s, the Hindus have nearly disappeared from the valley.

The political boundaries of Kashmir on occasion extended much beyond the valley. According to the Chinese traveler Xuanzang (earlier spelt Hiuen Tsang), the adjacent territories to the west and south down to the plains were also under the direct control of the king.

The jostling of the Kashmiri State within the circle of the north Indian powers led to an important political innovation. The Viṣṇudharmottara Purāṇa, believed to have been written in Kashmir during the rule of the Kārkoṭa kings, recommends innovations regarding the Rājasūya and the Aśvamedha sacrifices, of which the latter was responsible for much warfare amongst kings. It replaced these ancient rites by the rājyābhiṣeka (royal consecration) and surapratiṣṭhā (the fixing of the divine abode) rites.

Kashmir had a strong tradition of Sanskrit scholarship. Patañjali, the great author of the Mahābhāṣya, the commentary on Pāṇini's Aṣṭādhyāyī, was a Kashmiri. He is said to have made contributions also to Yoga and to Āyurveda (although some believe that there may have been more than one scholar with this name). Some take Bharata Muni of the Nāṭya Śāstra to be a Kashmiri.

The Yoga Vāsiṣṭha is a Kashmiri book with enduring influence on Indian thought. It may be viewed as a philosophical novel, and it has fascinating passages on time, space, matter and cognition. Starting with a position that seeks to unify space, time, matter, and consciousness, an argument is made in the book for relativity of space and time, cyclic and recursively defined universes, and a non-anthropocentric view.

Tantra: Śaivism and Vaiṣṇavism

The Kashmiri approach to the world is thorougly positive. It celebrates nature, and beauty in the objective world is taken as an attribute of divinity. It stresses the equivalence of the universe and the body and claims that the answer to the mystery of consciousness lies within the person. Although the Vaiṣṇavite Pāñcarātra now survives only in South India, its earliest teachers looked to Kashmir as the seat of learning and spiritual culture.

According to the historian Kalhaṇa, the worship of Śiva in Kashmir dates prior to the Mauryan King Aśoka. The Tantras were enshrined in texts known as the Āgamas, most of which are now lost. The pinnacle of the Tantric Śaiva tradition is the Trika system.

The philosophical ideas of recognition and vibration are central to Kashmir Śaivism. In the philosophy of recognition, it is proposed that the ultimate experience of enlightenment consists of a profound recognition that one's own true identity is that of Śiva. The doctrine of vibration speaks of the importance of experiencing *spanda*, the vibration or pulse of consciousness. All activities in the universe, including sensations, cognitions, and emotions ebb and flow as part of the universal rhythm of the one reality, Śiva.

In the first century, the Kuṣāṇ Emperor Kaniṣka chose Kashmir as the venue of a major Buddhist Council comprising of over 500 monks and scholars. At this meeting the previously unorganized portions of Buddha's discourses and the theoretical portions of the canon were codified. The entire canon (the Tripiṭaka) was inscribed on copper plates and deposited in a stupa.

Attracted by Kashmir's reputation as a center of scholarship, aspiring scholars from distant lands came to learn Sanskrit and to be trained as translators and teachers. Amongst these was Kumārajīva, the son of a Kashmiri who had married a princess in faraway Kucha. His mother later became a nun and she came to study in Kashmir and brought him along. He learnt the Mahāyāna scriptures from a famous teacher named Bandhudatta. Aftetr his education was complete, he returned to Kucha and later he helped establish the Chinese branch of the Mādhyamika, known as the San-lun, or "Three Treatises School."

According to some Tibetan sources, Nāropā and Padmasambhava (who introduced Tantric Buddhism into Tibet) were Kashmiris. The Tibetan script, which is derived from the Kashmiri Śāradā script, was brought into Tibet by Thonmi-Sambhota, who was sent to Kashmir during the reign of Durlabhavardhana to study with Devatītasiṃha.

———

The uniqueness of the Kashmiri idiom in artistic expression is well recognized by scholars. Lalitāditya built the Mārtaṇḍa temple and also an enormous caitya in the town of Parihāsapura which housed a giant Buddha. Only the plinth of this huge monument survives, although one of the paintings at Alchi is believed to be its representation. There was also an enormous stupa in Parihāsapura built by Lalitāditya's minister Caṅkuna, which may have been larger than the caitya. The Parihāsapura monuments became models for Buddhist architecture from Afghanistan to Japan.

The Paṇḍrethan temple and the Avantipura complex provide us further examples of the excellence of Kashmiri architecture and art. Kashmiri ivories and metal images are generally considered to be among the best anywhere in the world. Kashmir had a flourishing tradition of painting, which was put to use to decorate temple walls. The earliest surviving examples of these paintings come from Gilgit and date from about 8th century.

After Lalitāditya, Kashmiri style appears to have changed somewhat and endured till 10-11th century. The 9th century complex of Avantipura built by King Avantivarman is an amalgam of various earlier prevalent forms. The best example of this style is found in the bronzes cast by Kashmiri craftsmen for Tibetan patrons. The style of such bronzes presents a remarkable affinity to the wall-paintings dating to 10-11th century decorated in the Buddhist temples of Western Tibet.

One of the best sites to see the Kashmiri painting style is in the five temples comprising the dharma-maṇḍala at Alchi in Ladakh, which escaped destruction other Ladakhi temples suffered at the hands of a king who embraced Islam. The earliest of these buildings is the Du-khang where one can see astonishingly well preserved mandalas that document the Kashmiri Buddhist pantheon as well as the Buddhist representation of the Hindu pantheon.

According to the historian of art Susan Huntington, "Kashmir served as a source of imagery and influence for the northern and eastern movements of Buddhist art. The Yunkang caves in China, the wall paintings from several sites in Inner Asia, especially Qizil and Tun-huang, the paintings from the cache at Tun-huang, and some iconographic manuscripts from Japan, for example, should be evaluated with Kashmir in mind as a possible source. A full understanding of the transmission of Buddhist art through

Asia is dependent on developing a greater knowledge of Kashmiri art."

———

The 9th century scholar Ānandavardhana, a member of the court of King Avantivarman, wrote the Dhvanyāloka, the "Light of Suggestion," which is a world-class masterpiece of aesthetic theory. He rejected the earlier theories of alaṅkāra and guṇa by Bhāmaha and Daṇḍin according to which ornamental qualities and figures of speech distinguished poetry from ordinary speech. Ānandavardhana said that the difference was a quality called *dhvani* which communicates meaning by indirect suggestion.

Ānandavardhana was the first to note that rasa, identified by Bharata in his Nāṭya Śāstra as the essence of artistic expression, cannot be communicated directly. If one were to say that "so-and-so and his wife are very much in love," we fail to express the nature of the love. This can be done only by dhvani. Abhinavagupta, who lived about a hundred years after Ānandavardhana, added important elements to the dhvani theory. His famous commentary on the Dhvanyāloka is the Locana, and he also wrote on philosophy, poetry, tantra, and aesthetics. His book Tantrāloka (Light of the Tantras) is one of the most important on the subject. He also wrote a commentary on the Nāṭya Śāstra.

The massive thirteenth-century text Saṅgīta-ratnākara ("Ocean of Music and Dance"), composed by the Kashmiri theorist Śārṅgadeva, is an important landmark in Indian music history. A large part of this work is devoted to mārga, that is, the ancient music that includes the system of jātis and grāma-rāgas, and it mentions a total of 264 rāgas.

Kṣemendra was a philosopher, poet, and a pupil of Abhinavagupta. Among his books is the Bṛhat-kathāmañjari which is a summary of Gunāḍhya's Bṛhat-kathā in 7,500 stanzas. Somadeva's Kathā-sarit-sāgara is another version of Gunāḍhya's Bṛhat-kathā that influenced the birth of fiction in medieval times. These stories were written for Queen Sūryamatī, the wife of king Ananta (1028-1063).

The classic arts and the sciences of Kashmir came to an abrupt end when Islam became politically dominant in the fourteenth century. Sculpture, painting, dance, music could no longer be practiced. After the political situation had become stable, the subsequent centuries saw emphasis on devotion and its expression through the Kashmiri language as in the poetry of Lalleśvarī. The creative urges at the folk level found expression in the works of the craftsmen of wood and textiles.

But Kashmiri ideas lived on through the arts that transformed expression in Central and East Asia, and through Tantra and aesthetics they shaped attitudes in the rest of India. Many Kashmiris, like the musicologist Śārṅgadeva and the poet Bilhaṇa, emigrated. Although Kashmir had sunk to a state of misery, outsiders continued to pay homage to its memory as the land of learning, and Śāradā, its presiding goddess, became synonymous with Sarasvatī.

The major poets who followed Lalleśvarī include Habba Khatun, and the twentieth-century poets Mahjur, Abdul Ahad Azad, and Zinda Kaul. Habba Khatun is credited with originating the *lol* style of poetry where the predominant mood is that of longing and romantic love.

The theory and philosophy behind Kashmiri classical music called Sufiyana music was described in two books from the 17th and the 18th centuries, written in Persian: the anonymous Karāmat-e mujra (The Flowering of Munificence), and Daya Ram Kachroo Khushdil's Tarānā-e-Sarūr (The Song of Joy).

I got to visit the ruins of the Mārtaṇḍa Temple on the Mattan Karewa, built by Emperor Lalitāditya, many times. Built of stone, it is characterized by the simplicity of its conception: it is rectangular in plan, consisting of a maṇḍapa and a shrine. Two other shrines flank the maṇḍapa. It is enclosed by a vast courtyard by a peristyle wall with 84 secondary shrines in it. The columns of the peristyle are fluted.

Each of the 84 niches originally contained an image of a form of Sūrya. The number 84, as 21×4, appears to have been derived from the numerical association of 21 with the sun. It must have looked like a jeweled treasure on the plateau over Anantnag.

Kashmir became a princely state in the British Empire in 1846 after the First Anglo-Sikh war. A hundred years later, the movement for independence in British India spilled over to Kashmir. The Maharaja appeared to hold out for independence in August 1947 when India was partitioned. But in late October of that year Pakistani tribesmen, led by military officers in civilian clothes, tried to take the Vale by force. The Maharaja now joined the Indian Union, and soldiers of the Indian Army were flown into Srinagar which turned the tide of the invasion. The war raged throughout 1948. Finally, under the supervision of the United Nations a cease fire was declared on 1 January 1949. Pakistan controls about one-third of the Jammu and Kashmir State, mostly the northwest parts of Jammu, Baltistan, and the Gilgit region.

3. BEGINNINGS

We belong to the Razdan (Sanskrit *Rājānaka*) clan, known for both scholarship and war. The name Kak is believed to be an honorific, given to an ancestor who became the disciple of a sadhu (respectfully called *Kak*). There is mention in Kalhaṇa's Rājataraṅginī of a general, Tilak Kak, who came out at the losing end in the civil war during the reigns of Uccala and Sussala (c. 1100). Tradition has it that ours was one of the few Hindu families left in the valley during the oppressive regime of Sikandar (1389-1413).

Like most people, the Kaks believe that their lineage is ancient but had fallen on hard times. Father was orphaned early in his childhood and raised by an uncle and later by an older brother in the Punjab. The family's connection with the region was not recent because father's grandfather, Thakur Kak, went to Jhelum City in search for work in his youth before eventually returning to Srinagar.

Prior to the introduction of modern professions, life in Kashmir was centered on agriculture, which was organized under the system of kārdārī. The collection of agricultural tax from the peasants was contracted out to the kārdār, who would collect half the produce, pay the taxes due to the governor and keep the rest to himself. When the crops failed, the kārdār was at the mercy of the governor or his agent. The good ruler let the kārdār carry the debt to the next year or even forgive it; the bad ruler used the occasion to unleash tyranny.

In the stagnant economy of the late 18th and early 19th centuries, ravaged by unsettled conditions and continuing war in India, the name of the game for powerful families in Kashmir was the kārdār position. In spite of its risks it offered much reward.

During 1754-1762, while the Durrani king Ahmad Shah was busy raiding north India, the governor Raja Sukh Jivan declared independence. Ahmad Shah sacked Delhi in 1757 and then defeated the Marathas in the Third Battle of Panipat in 1761. In 1762, he turned to Kashmir, wresting it back from Sukh Jivan.

Shah Timur was the ruler of Kabul from 1772 to 1793. The Afghans chieftains were quarrelsome and Timur was not as strong as his father. He left twenty four sons and once the dust had settled on the succession process, Shah Zaman succeeded him.

An ancestor in the Kak family, Mukund Kak (approx 1776-1847), who was a kārdār, was put in prison and his houses demolished when his rival complained to the governor about the misappropriation of the revenue collected in his district. He was freed when his friend Trinayan Kaul paid off the governor. Mukund and Trinayan sealed their friendhip by the marriage of their children, Sataram Kak (c. 1805-1845) and Gangā Devi, and after this the two families emigrated.

During the late 18th century, new political and military forces were emerging. The Durrani ruler Shah Zaman appointed a young Sikh, Ranjit Singh, as governor of the Punjab, who declared independence in 1801, soon becaming the preeminent king of the region. The British were by now a powerful force and they induced the Iranians to attack Zaman who lost and was blinded and imprisoned.

In 1803, eighteen year old Shah Shuja became the king of Afghanistan. In 1809, he was overthrown and took refuge in Ranjit Singh's court. He was asked by Ranjit Singh to take a force to Kashmir but lost the battle and was taken prisoner. The Afghan governor, Azim Khan, now handed him over to Ranjit Singh who kept him jailed from 1813 to 1814. To gain his freedom, Shah Shuja gave the Kohinoor diamond to the Maharaja.

––––––

The story of the kārdārs Mirza Pandit Dhar and his nephew Birbal Dhar in freeing Kashmir from the oppression of the Afghans is well remembered. The crops had failed and Birbal Dhar couldn't collect the one hundred thousand rupees that were due to Azim Khan, governor during 1810-1816, who had defeated Shah Shuja. The governor sent 100 soldiers to arrest Birbal Dhar.

Mirza Pandit gave a bond to Azim Khan that he would pay Birbal Dhar's debt but he advised his nephew to escape to Lahore and urge Ranjit Singh to intervene.

Birbal Dhar was advised by Vasakak Harkarabashi to leave his wife and daughter-in-law with his friend Qudus Gojawari for safety. Birbal did this and then with his son left for Lahore on horseback. When Azim Khan found that Birbal was missing he asked Mirza Pandit Dhar what had happened. Mirza Pandit told him that Birbal had either gone on a pilgrimage or to Lahore to get the Sikhs against him. When asked what should be done next, Mirza Pandit said that he, namely Mirza Pandit, should be put to death and Birbal's debts charged to him.

The dialogue between Azim Khan and Mirza Pandit went as follows (as recounted in Anand Koul's *The Kashmiri Pandit*):

Azim: Birbal kujā raft (Where has Birbal gone?)

Mirza Pandit: Hargāh au rā hawas-i-dunyā na munda bāshad ba Gangā khwāhad raft warnah peshi Ranjit rafta Singhān bar tu ārad (Should he care no more for the world he will go to the Ganga; otherwise, he will go to Ranjit and bring the Singhs against you.)
Azim: Pas chi salāh (What advice then?)
Mirza Pandit: Kushtani Mirzā Pandit (Putting Mirza Pandit to death.)
Azim: Bākayāt-i-Birbal? (The debt of Birbal?)
Mirza Pandit: Ba pāyi Mirza Pandit (To be paid by Mirza Pandit.)

The tyrant was so impressed by Mirza Pandit's brave words that he left him alone but imposed a daily fine of 1000 rupees on Vasakak Harkarabashi to pressure him to reveal the whereabouts of Birbal Dhar's wife and daughter-in-law. This continued for nine days.

Vasakak was in a bind. He had given word that he would keep the whereabouts of Birbal's wife and daughter-in-law secret. On the other hand, the daily fine, if continued longer, would bring his family to ruin. His relatives were distraught. Birbal Dhar's son-in-law Tilak Chand Munshi found out from his wife where the ladies were and informed the governor.

Azim pounced on this opportunity to destroy Birbal's family. The two ladies were arrested and brought to his compound by boat. Birbal Dhar's wife took poison and killed herself, and the daughter-in-law was sent to Kabul to the King's harem. Vasakak Harkarabashi was put to death for not having assisted Azim in finding the ladies.

Azim Khan installed his younger brother Jabbar Khan as governor and returned to Afghanistan in 1816 with a loot of 20 million rupees. Egged on by Birbal Dhar's promise to pay for losses if the Sikhs did not win, and keeping his son

Raj Kak Dhar as guarantee, Ranjit Singh now sent an army to liberate Kashmir.

Jabbar was defeated and Kashmir became a province of the Punjab in 1819. The first Sikh governor was Diwan Moti Ram with Birbal Dhar as peshkar, or principal adviser. The administration in Kashmir was conducted in Persian and the peshkar's job included translating the Diwan's orders.

The officers working for the peshkar were called the ahalkārs, and when the peshkar lost his job so did they. There was much incentive for those out of power to bring down the peshkar for life for the ambitious in 19th century Kashmir was a zero-sum game.

After a year, Birbal Dhar, and his uncles Mirza Pandit Dhar and Sahaj Ram Dhar were invited to attend Ranjit Singh's Darbar. Mirza Pandit Dhar died on the way of cholera and his brother Sahaj Ram Dhar decided to retire from active life. Birbal Dhar proceeded to Lahore by himself and he was showered many honors by the Maharaja.

When Birbal Dhar returned to Kashmir, he didn't properly acknowledge his cousin, Ram Dhar, Sahaj Ram Dhar's son, who had come to receive him. Hurt by this slight, Ram Dhar went to the governor, complaining that Birbal Dhar was conspiring with the Rajas of Muzaffarabad against the Sikhs. The governor and Birbal Dhar soon fell out and Birbal Dhar was dismissed and Ram Dhar's brother Ganesh Dhar was appointed peshkar in his place.

The Kaks

Amar Nath Kak (1888-1963), in his autobiography *Hamārā Vṛttānta*, provides another sidelight to the story that pits the Bhan and the Kak families against each other. When the Sikhs seized Kashmir, Trinayan Kaul and Sataram Kak returned and in due course Sataram became the kārdār of Anantnag district. Birbal Dhar's daughter was married into the Bhan family, and one of their young men had a falling out with his brother and he decided to go to Lahore to plead his case. He had to pass through Sataram Kak's district on this journey, but Sataram prevented him from doing so.

The young man now vowed to ruin Sataram. In due course he became a high official and he schemed to impose a fine of 100,000 rupees on Sataram. Like his father's before him, Sataram's properties were seized and he was put in prison, dying of cholera in the epidemic of 1845, leaving behind his wife, four sons, and two daughters.

Sataram Kak's youngest son Govind Kak (1844-1904) wrote a version of the Mahābhārata in Persian. Govind Kak was the grandfather of Ram Chandra Kak (1893-1983) who was a pioneering archaeologist, author of books on Kashmir antiquities, and prime minister of Jammu and Kashmir during 1945-1947.

The immediate ancestors of our branch of the Kak family are described in my father's autobiography (*Autumn Leaves*, 1995). Ram Chandra Kak's family is descended from Prabhakar, the second son to Sunda Kak (c. 1670), whereas ours descends from Raghav, the fourth son.

My link to the lived life of late 19th century Kashmir was through my granduncle Bayaji, Kishan Lal Kak, who became father's adoptive dad after he lost both his parents when young. Bayaji must have been born around 1890 or so. He was austere and disciplined, waking up before dawn, bathing under the tap in the yard, and then doing puja for several hours. He was an excellent chess player and he told us fascinating stories of his days in the militaty ancillary service in Abbottabad, Quetta, and Muzaffarabad.

My paternal grandmother's family was from Pulwama, a town I have not seen. My father told me that his grandfather emulated his relative by writing a version of the Rāmāyaṇa in Persian.

Father's father, Suraj Kak, was first-born, quick-tempered, independent, and resourceful. After some adventures, such as posing as a sadhu to capture a dreaded robber for a prize, he joined the police. To mail money to his family in Srinagar through an untrustworthy postal service, he was known to have cut currency notes in half and mailed the halves in separate envelopes, sending out the second after ensuring that the first had arrived. For the crook in the post office any one set would have been useless.

Father was the youngest of three sons. His mother, Siddhalakshmi, died in an epidemic (perhaps the worldwide influenza epidemic of 1918) before he turned one. He lost his father, killed in a police mission in the mountains, when he was about ten.

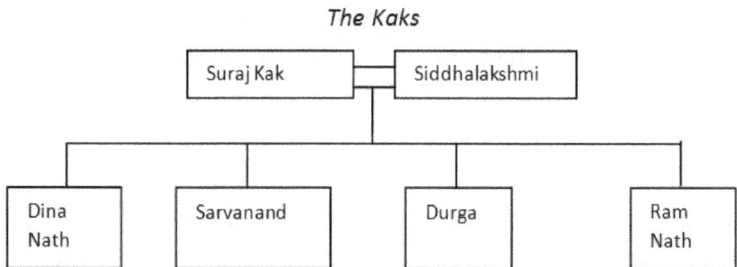

The Kaks

```
        ┌─────────────┐   ┌─────────────────┐
        │  Suraj Kak  │───│  Siddhalakshmi  │
        └─────────────┘   └─────────────────┘
   ┌──────────┬──────────────┼──────────────┬──────────┐
┌────────┐ ┌───────────┐ ┌─────────┐ ┌────────┐
│  Dina  │ │ Sarvanand │ │  Durga  │ │  Ram   │
│  Nath  │ │           │ │         │ │  Nath  │
└────────┘ └───────────┘ └─────────┘ └────────┘
```

For a few years, father hung around in the joint family house with the understanding that he was now the adoptive son of his youngest uncle and aunt, namely Bayaji and his wife Didda. Both were kind to him but when not around to speak up for him, he was beaten without mercy for some transgression or the other by relatives. After witnessing one of these beatings on a visit to Srinagar, his older brother, Babuji (Dina Nath), who had, by this time, become lecturer of philosophy in a college in Kapurthala in the Punjab, decided to take him there and put him in school.

The other brother, Sarvanand, had a degree in chemistry and he took a job with a chemical company in Kanpur and later in Bihar, and we did not see very much of him or his family. Durgā died giving birth to a child.

Babuji was a Gandhian and a strict disciplinarian who was uninterested in money and father modeled himself much after him. Babuji's wife, Bibiji, resented the fact that she had to bring up her young brother-in-law and this created tension in the family. Actually, father was not the only young man living with them and the others were not even relatives. This would happen when a village boy came to study at Babuji's college and if he had no place to stay, Babuji would offer to have him live at home during the period of study.

Father's character was molded by his efforts to become a serious yoga adept. He trained as a veterinarian in Lahore, in what is now Pakistan, and was thereupon appointed a doctor in the Jammu and Kashmir Veterinary Department. His postings, generally of two-year duration, took him to far corners of the state. His serious training in yoga took place in Reasi, a town in Jammu. His teacher was his landlord, Jyoti Prakash Kalia, who was by profession a lawyer.

Father was also interested in deeper questions on the nature of reality. He read widely and was excellent at languages, speaking Hindi, Urdu, Punjabi, Dogri, and other local languages without accent.

The Karihaloos

The Karihaloo name is a nickname that stuck with one of the Kaul families of Kashmir. It is believed that their ancestor, who was the first to be called by this nickname, was a courtier in the Mughal court of Emperor Farrukhsiyar.

When Aurangzeb died in 1707 at the end of a long reign, there were seventeen claimants to the throne, including sons, grandsons and great grandsons. The sons fought a pitched battle near Agra; Prince Muazzam prevailed and assumed the title Bahadur Shah I. Another son entered the fight a year later and was killed. Bahadur Shah was well in his sixties when he took control of the empire, dying five years later.

Bahadur Shah's son Jahandar Shah, who succeeded him, was a womanizing drunk whose mistress Lal Kunwar took full advantage of the emperor's condition and enriched herself and her family. Jahandar Shah was murdered in 1713 and then Bahadur's grandson Farrukhsiyar ascended the throne. He was helped by two brothers named Sayyid, generals belonging to old aristocracy, who tried to reduce the emperor to a figurehead.

Farrukhsiyar struggled to curb the power of the Sayyid brothers without much success. Taking advantage of the situation, the Rajputs, the Jats, and the Sikhs rose in revolt. It was during his reign in 1717 that the East India Company bought duty-free trading rights in Bengal for mere 3,000 rupees, which aided the British in later years to establish firm foothold in India.

The Sayyids remained powerful, but Farrukhsiyar at long last schemed to send away one of them to the South while the other was kept under constant watch in Delhi. The brother in Deccan colluded with the Marathas and they attacked Delhi. The emperor was seized, blinded and later poisoned and stabbed to death.

After deposing Farrukhsiyar, the Sayyid brothers continued as kingmakers and placed on the throne Rafi-ul-Darajat. He was soon deposed and replaced by his elder brother, Rafi-ud-Daula. After the death of the latter, the brothers appointed as emperor Muhammad Shah (r.1719-1749) who was another grandson of Bahadur Shah I. Sometime after this the Sayyid brothers were murdered.

It was in Muhammad Shah's rule that the Kashmiri Jai Ram Bhan obtained the assent of the emperor that the Kashmiri Hindus be addressed as "Pandit" rather than "Khwajah", the term previously employed.

The dying days of the Mughal Empire were a great time for ambitious people to make their fortune in Delhi. The large Kashmiri community in the court included one Dattatreya Kaul, an ancestor to the Karihaloos. His exalted station entitled him to be carried around in a palanquin (as was the custom for the aristocracy), and as he would have to crane his neck out to see people, the Kashmiris who are notorious for inventing nicknames starting calling him Karihaloo (*kar* = neck, *haloo* = crooked), and the name stuck.

After the ascendancy of the British and the start of the Dogra rule in the valley, the Karihaloos of Delhi returned to Kashmir. The most recent forefather of the Karihaloos was Prasad, who was a Mushrimal in the Shali Store, a sort of a clerk, in the late 1800s. His wife's name was Deva Mali and they had five sons — Govind, Dama (c. 1890-1952), Nanda, Sham and Soda — and 3 daughters, Kujamal, Madhumati and Lakshmi. Prasad's eldest son, the saintly Govind, seemed to have had premonition of early death at twenty-one.

Prasad was a simple man who had complete faith in God. He was transferred to some place outside Srinagar, where he died of what was then thought to be cholera. His body was brought back in a boat, and it was discovered that he had kept twenty five rupees on his person for death-rites.

After Govind's death, Dama Kaul took up a job in the stationery department. Eventually, other sons of Prasad also found jobs. Nand Kaul joined post office, retiring as deputy

31

postmaster. Sham Kaul, after completing his medical training in India, went to England for higher studies for five years. On his return, he joined the government hospital where he rose to the post of the chief tuberculosis officer. He was westernized, and in his appearance looked quite the Englishman. Soda Kaul joined government secretariat as a clerk.

The family moved to a large compound in Fateh Kadal. In addition to the main house, where the family lived, there were two other houses for servants, storerooms, teacher room, and so on. Dama Kaul, being the eldest brother, was in charge of the family finances and the three younger brothers were obedient to him. He was a dynamic person who believed in good life and unity of the family.

Sham Kaul purchased a maroon-colored Chevrolet, one of the first private cars in Kashmir, and joined the exclusive Amar Singh Club. The house had a beautiful garden, one portion of which was for growing kitchen vegetables and flowers, and the other was called "tennis ground" where the children played badminton. The garden had two big pine trees, one cherry tree, one apricot tree, and a grape vine.

The boys and girls spent an idyllic childhood playing in the garden and doing other things children do. Sometimes the girls would climb the cherry tree to hide from the tutor as he made his rounds.

A few years later, Dama Kaul resigned his job in the stationery department to try his luck in motor-parts business in Bombay. Accompanied by Soda Kaul and a servant, he rented a shop. The business did well, but then a dispute arose over how the profits were to be divided. The joint family came to an end, and the brothers went their ways, and the house in Fateh Kadal was sold.

Dama Kaul now bought a house in Mandir Bagh in Srinagar. His wife Deva Mali was very sick in her later years.

She developed an infection when operated upon for tonsils with a rusted instrument. Later, this turned into cancer on her face and throat and she lived through several years of great pain, dying in 1950.

Mother was born Chuni to Dama Kaul and Deva Mali in March 1929. She was the fifth surviving child of a total of six. She had two older brothers, Kashi Nath and Radha Krishan, two older sisters, Kamla (or Kamala) and Aruna, and one younger brother, Makhan Lal; one older sibling, Dhruva, suffocated to death under piles of bedding and blankets in the chaos of a family wedding.

The girls attended the Mission school. They were taken out of the school after a scandalous event when a Kashmiri girl from a respectable family eloped with her teacher. Everything was carefully planned for the elopement: she left some of her hair and goat's blood in the room to fake kidnapping. She and her lover were eventually traced to Bombay. Owing to the disapproval of the girl's behavior by his parents, the young man now refused to marry her.

The Karihaloo-Kauls

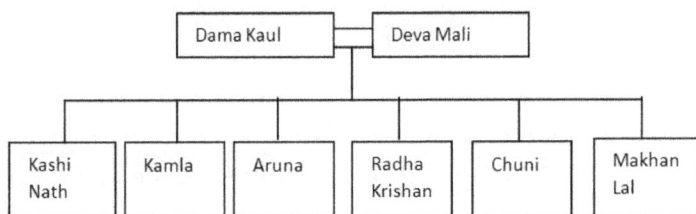

| Dama Kaul | Deva Mali |

| Kashi Nath | Kamla | Aruna | Radha Krishan | Chuni | Makhan Lal |

The upshot of this scandal was that many parents, including Dama Kaul, decided to home-school the girls. This is how my mother's childhood had little formal schooling and much play in the family compound.

33

Shoklam karith hyotay vanavoenuy
Rut phal dyutay maaji Bhavaanae

Invoking the Lord we begin our chant
Mother Bhavāni has given us boon.
—Henzae chant at wedding

Mother was married to my father in the winter of 1944, before she turned 15. Marriage of a girl that age was typical of those times. It was marriage of two families with somewhat different values. The Kauls (Karihaloos) were a professional family devoted to good life and material success. The Kaks stressed austerity and understatement and they maintained, or wished to maintain, some connection to Sanskrit learning. In appearance these two families were like the two complementary and oppositional poles of the Hindu belief system related to the man-in-the-world and the renouncer, which are the worlds of Viṣṇu and Śiva, respectively.

The Kauls were Bhānamāsi who ate meat during the all-important Śivarātri celebrations whereas the Kaks were Malamāsi who remained vegetarian during this period. This distinction had something to do with the belief of the Kaks that they were one of the eleven families that had survived the genocide and expulsion of the Hindus in the late 1300s.

These eleven families had held on to their ancient customs while the Bhānamāsi were descended from the families that returned during a later prosperous period but in the process adopted new customs, especially related to calendric calculations for festivals.

Mother added to the positive energy of the Kauls with the relentless urge of the Kaks to excel. She was fun-loving, and she liked visiting places, organizing picnics, cooking and entertaining people at home, but behind her friendly nature lay steely resolve. Her fearlessness and independence of spirit came perhaps from the many years she spent fighting for her space with older cousins and siblings.

My parents saw each other for the first time on the wedding day. Kashmiris had the custom of giving a new name to the girl on her marriage and the elders of the Kak family chose Satyavati, whereas father picked Sarojini, which became her official name.

A few months after the wedding, father and mother went to Kapurthala to see Babuji's family. On this trip they also saw her sister Aruna and her husband, Zinda Lal, in Muzaffarabad and her older brother Kashi Nath in Lahore. Babuji treated mother like a daughter-in-law and his daughters, Hem and Asha, became fond of her. The Punjab, and its glittering capital Lahore, was an entirely new world to her. Here people spoke different languages and there was wealth and technology, such as trains, she had not seen before.

Father brought her books to learn Hindi, Sanskrit, and English. She knew Urdu very well. During their stay outside Kashmir, she learnt to speak Dogri and Punjabi, and in Leh, she picked up rudimentary Ladakhi.

This was the time most Kashmiri lived by the cycle of festivals, fasts and celebrations, and this cycle kept my parents busy. There was something happening every week with special observances on the full moon, the new moon and other days specified in the lunar almanac. In the month of Māgh, which fell in winter, father and mother would set out at dawn, covered in blankets, to the temple spring to take a dip. The family priest showed up at home from time to time to look at the horoscopes and on special days such as birthdays.

The main celebrations were those of Herath (Hararātri or Śivarātri) on the thirteenth night of Phālgun,

35

Yakṣa Amāvasya, Navreh (or the New Year) on the first bright fortnight of Caitra, Jyeṣṭha Aṣṭamī when the Kṣīra Bhavānī fair is held, Rakhri on the full-moon day of Śrāvaṇa, Janma Aṣṭamī on the eighth day of the dark fortnight of Bhādrapada, and Pan on Gaṇeśa Caturthī.

Some of my most magical childhood memories are of Śivarātri at our ancestral home in Srinagar when, half-asleep in the early hours of the morning, we kept vigil, chanting *Om Namah Śivāya*. Every Janma Aṣṭamī, mother would decorate a swing with the picture of the baby Kṛṣṇa and we would wait until the stroke of midnight to mark his birth. Mother always prepared *roth* on Pan and we all looked forward to eating this sweetened bread.

> *bel tai madel vena golaab pamposh das tai*
> *poozai lagas param ŚivasŚivanathas tai*
>
> *Bel leaves, mint, rose and lilies in my hands*
> *I offer in puja to Param Śiva, Śivanath*
> – Krishna Joo Razdan

Song and music were a large element of our celebrations. At the weddings the formal beginning was marked by a chant called *henzae* set to the ancient Sāmavedic meter, which told the story of the wedding of Śiva and Pārvatī. The ladies touched the forehead of other women guests with auspicious *isaband* seeds that were then dropped in Kangris where they broke open in the fire producing the most wonderful fragrance.

At home no subject was taboo, and we could present our opinions freely and challenge visitors, so long it was done respectfully. Similar free discussions took place in the homes of relatives and friends.

Due to frequent transfers, father's box of books remained behind in Srinagar and I could lay my hands on these only during vacations or other visits to the city. Ordinarily all one got to read were the textbooks, the occasional magazine, and the daily newspaper.

Our ancestral house was built by my grandfather Suraj Kak at Sathu Barbarshah, a district of Srinagar that joined Habbakadal at one end and Dalgate at the other. Usually, the day after reaching Srinagar on vacations, we headed early in the morning for the Shankarāchārya Temple atop the thousand-foot hill that commands the city.

In the Sathu house, the fourth floor was locked up due to litigation. The house was narrow with length that was about three-times of width. The ground floor was the divān, the living room, with one-third of it backing to the street that served as the kitchen in the traditional Kashmiri fashion, with open fire stove. Originally, piped water came only to a faucet in the backyard that overlooked the Tsunthkol (a waterway that joins the Vyeth — Vitasta or Jhelum River — and the Dal Lake). Later, an extension from the street was brought into the kitchen.

The house was dark, and at night the voltage was low. The valley then was served by a small and ancient hydroelectric power station. It was nearly impossible to read in the dim light of the bulb in the room, so we would sit around on the floor at different places against the wall, and talk or just listen. Everyone retired by ten.

I could not speak Kashmiri with fluency. I recall not answering when Didda (who did not speak Hindi) spoke to me. The adults laughed good-naturedly at my reserve. They thought I was a sensitive, brooding child.

My older cousins (Babuji's daughters), one of whom was already married, made fun of my shyness. When I wasn't reading or playing with other kids, I remained detached, observing people and things.

4. CHILDHOOD

Mother's first child arrived in October 1944. By the time she was 25, she had five children: Avinash, me, Shakti, Jaishree, and Neeraj. During the war with Pakistan, when there was fear that the Hindus will be killed, Babuji persuaded father and mother to send Avinash out of Kashmir to live with him. Since Babuji didn't have a son, and mother by that time had two, it was the understanding that Avinash would be adopted, as during those times such adoptions within the family were common. But Babuji was soon to learn that Bibiji was opposed to the idea and Avinash made his unhappiness so clear that he returned home after a couple years.

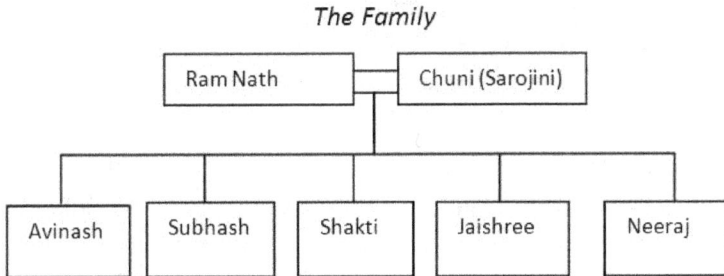

The Family

```
        ┌─────────────┬─────────────────┐
        │  Ram Nath   │ Chuni (Sarojini)│
        └─────────────┴─────────────────┘
                       │
   ┌───────┬───────────┼───────────┬───────────┐
┌──────┐┌────────┐┌────────┐┌──────────┐┌────────┐
│Avinash││Subhash ││ Shakti ││ Jaishree ││ Neeraj │
└──────┘└────────┘└────────┘└──────────┘└────────┘
```

Around the time Neeraj was born, the government was beginning to push the concept of family planning. Mother liked the idea but couldn't get father to discuss it. So she took the matter in her own hands and, with ten-year old Avinash in tow, approached a lady doctor-relative in Srinagar to perform the tubal procedure.

The visits to the ancestral house in Sathu Barbarshah in Srinagar ceased after Didda passed away in 1962 and Bayaji went to live with his older daughter, Kamalā, in Ghaziabad, near Delhi. We saw Babuji and Bibiji and their married children only on their infrequent visits to Kashmir, so the relatives we were closest to were from mother's side of the family.

For years, father was transferred from one small town to another. After this, he had an extended posting of six years or so in Anantnag and thereupon postings at Cheshmashahi on the Dal Lake and in Srinagar, and his last posting was in Jammu. After he retired from the veterinary service he consulted with the State Bank for a few years.

Like Bayaji, father was an early riser, and he took his bath with cold water, no matter what the temperature, followed by meditation and daily chanting of Sanskrit stotras. On holidays, he spent the day reading newspapers or a book and in the evening he went out for a walk if there were no visitors. When we had visitors, they had to be served tea and snacks, and the children were expected to make small talk.

Mother rose later, and did her stotras that she had learnt from father both morning and evening. She also recited Hindi and Kashmiri bhajans and at the end of the puja she waved the lit ratnadīp lamp at the pictures of the deities. She did this routine no matter what, even when she was ill.

With five children and no heating in the house, there was much to be done. In winter, sometimes the water pipes froze and then she, or the children, had to take the dishes down to the open yard and wash them under the running street tap.

In the morning the mattresses were piled up in a corner, and at night they were spread out with sheets and covers laid on top of them. Mother did all work without complaint. The children helped out mostly with the beds and visits to the bazaar to buy groceries.

My earliest recollections go back to isolated events in Basohli, Bilawar, and Kathua. One image is of the family crossing a raging river by raft, protected by ropes held by people at the bank.There was a flawed transfer of the rope to the other bank, and we narrowly survived being swept down the river.One evening a snake slithered up the wooden frame of the cot on which I lay asleep. When discovered, there was uproar and the snake was chased out. My first school was in Kathua, and I recallbeing in Srinagar at my sick maternal grandfather's home.

1951

We went by bus from Kathua to Udhampur. The bus had a door at the back and bench seating that ran parallel to the length. The driver's assistant, called cleaner, cranked the engine and added water to the radiator when necessary. I can picture my older brother Avinash and I standing in the bus looking excitedly beyond the turns of the road and wondering what Udhampur would be like. My sister Shakti was still just a few months old and she traveled sitting in mother's lap.

Udhampur, in the low hills beyond the edge of the plains, is extremely hot. The sunlight was blinding in summer, and we spent sleepless nights in the heat with the cries of the town chowkidars repeating *jāgate raho, hoshiyār*.

A political party named the Prajā Parishad began agitating for full integration of the statewith India and after some weeks Udhampur was placed under curfew and the army called in. After things had calmed down a bit, father and I walked through the shuttered bazaar with Gurkha soldiers in full gear standing guard at street corners. I saw my first movie, Anarkali, in Udhampur and I was perplexed by what I thought was a disjointed sequence of images on the screen.

Two siblings arrived in Udhampur: Jaishree and Neeraj. I had a classmate named Neeraj that I was impressed by and I asked father to give that name to the new boy.

I was an exceedingly shy child. When we moved into rented rooms where the courtyard was shared with the landlord's family, no one heard me speak or utter a sound. After several months the landlord told my father how sorry he was that one of his children, namely I, was mute.

Perhaps the reason behind my shyness was my stammer, which took me some years to overcome. I don't know if being made to write with right hand was responsible for the stammer because I doubt I am naturally left-handed although I use the left hand for some tasks.

Avinash was extroverted and articulate, and very good at studies. He was also thoughtful and far ahead of boys of his age in awareness of social issues. As brothers not far removed in age, we had our fights.

In spite of being quiet, or perhaps because of it, I was fascinated by language and meaning. In second grade in Udhampur, I mulled for hours over why some words have different meaning in different contexts. I was perplexed by *lagna*, because it could mean different things such as to "get hurt", "to feel", "to be attached", "to fix", "auspicious time", and a specific "ritual". Just a small change in emphasis could alter the meaning from "reality" to "illusion" in going from *brahma* to *bhrama*.

1954

After Udhampur we were in Kulgam for two years. The first year we lived in a second floor apartment at the bazaar and then moved into newly constructed housing for the veterinary staff at the edge of the town, in the direction of River Veshiv.

When I was seven I had a very vivid dream that was to impact me greatly. In this dream I saw myself die, with the assembled relatives preparing my body for the funeral, which was then carried away to the cremation ground. While the dream was unfolding in a most lucid manner, I felt no emotion and just watched things happen as if I was apart from everything.

This dream stayed with me for years. I was so fearful of seeing it again that I willed myself not to remember anything on waking up, and I kept up with this resolve for nearly ten years.

Somewhat around this time father told me a property of the mind that has been confirmed by recent science and my own meditation practice. I asked father why was it that I saw myself falling into an abyss in my dream. With his insights from years of yogic practice, he said it was because I was perhaps lying on my back with one foot over another, and as the foot slipped, the mind made up a script with the corresponding fall. The key idea, he said, was that the mind is just a tad behind the goings on in the body.

Modern neuroscience has shown that the conscious mind does lag the processes in the brain by a few hundred milliseconds. In volitional acts, the activity in the brain precedes by a similar period the moment the individual believes the decision was made.

Having gone through a spiritual apprenticeship in his youth, father was keen to meet saints, of whom there were many in all parts of the state. When transferred to a new town, he would pay at least one visit to the local saint, but he kept his distance for he believed some of them were cantankerous. Just like the political administration, these saints had divided up the state into different districts. There were some who spoke in riddles; others who foretold the future; some lived in remote villages and never traveled; while others were on continual tour with retinue of hangers-on.

Another memory from this period is of near drowning in a pond in the water garden of Nishat Bagh where a stranger pulled me out of the water.

When I was eight, I came down with a bad case of typhoid. The temperature would not let up for days and I wasted into a skeleton. Finally, after four weeks, the temperature broke. I was so weak that I had to literally learn to crawl and walk.

While convalescing, I fell in the kitchen fire at the stove on the floor in a spell of dizziness and burnt my left hand rather badly. When we moved to Baramulla, northwest of Srinagar in 1956, the hand had not yet healed.

1956

We were in Baramulla, the town nearest the cease-fire line with Pakistan, for just over a year. There was talk that tribesmen from across the border were planning to sneak into the valley for another round of war. Mother now refused to live in the secluded house that was to be father's official residence. She didn't feel safe and she said she would rather live on the compound of the veterinary hospital with just one living room, which also served as bedroom, and kitchen.

It was common to see convoys of military vehicles pass our home. Tensions with Pakistan rose in January 1957 until before 26 January for two nights there was a constant stream of Army trucks. The word in the bazaar was that they were sent to relieve the soldiers but by choosing the time when the attack was expected the maneuver doubled the strength at the border, which forestalled the attack.

It took me months to recover from the weakness caused by typhoid, and I suffered for months from severe rheumatic pain all over my body.

1957

Next year, father was transferred to Leh in Ladakh. At 11,500 feet, this place is much colder than Kashmir. The road to Ladakh from Srinagar was yet to be completed but Leh had an airport and military planes had airlifted jeeps for use in the vast Ladakh district. There was no civilian air service but the military would let civilian passengers on their flights when they had free seats.

Father, twelve-year old Avinash and ten-year old I flew in a Dakota. Our task was to help out father with the cooking which taught us responsibility but we were mighty relieved when mother arrived a couple months later with the other children.

We had come to Leh in summer, when the climate is very pleasant. But soon it started getting cold and we were outfitted in Ladakhi clothes that afforded more protection than Kashmiri dress.

Our school, which was co-educational, was just behind our home. Its principal was the widely respected and dignified Eliezer Joldan. The school was well run and in pleasant weather classes were sometimes held under the trees.

In winter, when extended bad weather made it impossible for cargo planes to land on the Leh airstrip, boxes would be air dropped. Sometimes, when the planes did not find favorable conditions for the drop, they circled for fifteen minutes or so before returning to base.

Father and mother went through a phase when they read a lot of Urdu fiction. I was intrigued and taught myself the script to find out what the books were about. I picked up rudimentary Ladakhi and still remember Ladakhi numbers.

In winters, there were many parties and reading of romances. As there was no heating in the drafty house, we huddled together for warmth. Once mother had excruciating pain in her teeth. There was no qualified dentist in town and the person who was called pulled out her molars without anesthesia.

Our parents were friends with the Safayas and the Kashkaris. Dr Gopi Nath Safaya was father's colleague and Dr Som Nath Kashkari was the medical doctor. Card games were popular and the children got to join in. Dr Kashkari's daughter, Veena, who was about the same age as my sister Shakti, became a constant playmate. She was to become a doctor like her father, but died young in a tragic family situation.

Dr Safaya's son, Pradeep (or Deep), was about my age. Later, I also became friends with Deep's older brothers, and on many occasions I was to stay at their home in Safakadal in Srinagar.

Many years later in the United States, Pradeep and his American wife became successful entrepreneurs and at one point during the tech bubble of the late 90s they were the richest family in Colorado. Dr Kashkari's nephew, Neel, got to run the Troubled Asset Relief Program (TARP) —the U.S. government's response to the financial crisis of 2007–08 — as Assistant Secretary of the Treasury for Financial Stability from October 2008 to May 2009 in the Bush and Obama Administrations. He ran for Governor of California in the 2014 election, but lost to the incumbent Jerry Brown, and currently he is President of the Federal Reserve Bank of Minneapolis.

———

1959

After Leh, we were back in the valley in the city of Anantnag. Here one could subscribe to Delhi newspapers and magazines which we read literally by the line. Father arranged for me a membership of the Town Committee Library and I read the entire collection of European and Indo-Anglian fiction and history books such as Churchill's six-volume history of the Second World War. English, French and Russian novels were my favorites and I also read biography and Indian and world history.

I also borrowed extensively from the library at college at Anantnag. This opened the window on history of science and ideas and it is then I first came across Bertrand Russell and Ludwig Wittgenstein.

I wrote my first verse in Leh in Hindi when I was about 11 years old. It was written in the *dohā* style of medieval poetry. Later in Anantnag I wrote long poems and fiction, which I continued during my engineering studies at Srinagar.

In Anantnag, father's hospital had two resident breeding bulls that had lived as companions for several years and now one was sent to another town. When the truck left with the departing bull, tears rolled down the cheeks of the one left behind. It was moving to learn that animals were not all that different from us.

Encouraged by my own writing projects, mother started writing notes on her childhood in a notebook she called *Patthar Ke Dil* (Hearts of Stone). But this was so ridiculed by a relative, who believed in keeping things within the family, that she tore it up.

———

In the Valley, we spent weeks during the summer and winter holidays in Srinagar at our ancestral home. I didn't know anyone and mainly loitered in the bazaar, or accompanied mother in her shopping to carry bags and to check the shopkeepers' arithmetic. In the evenings, I sometimes ran alone to Dalgate to see the boats being transferred across the lock that joined the lake to the river. By the time I returned, the lights of the houseboats shimmered in the water and the breeze billowed out my shirt and lightened my steps.

In late autumn, we burnt chinar leaves to make charcoal for the kāngaris. Once the snow settled on the ground we were mainly cloistered indoors. Wrapped in a blanket in my own corner of the divān, I listened to the gossip of the women as they prepared the samāvār for salted shīrchai and sweet kehva. In the evenings, the men narrated their work stories. We children knew every social and office scandal.

In ten years of schooling in six different towns, the weather varied from tropical to arctic. In the hills, it was common to see cases of possession and bewitchment. Sometimes the possessed person was brought by relatives to father for treatment, but he would explain his inability to help.

To help the cause of national integration, father decreed that the children will speak Hindi at home. As we had older relatives who spoke only Kashmiri, the children became fluent in both languages. I took my father's command literally and, being shy, did not speak Kashmiri as often as I should have.

Mother spoke to us mostly in Kashmiri, as did our relatives. In Jammu the bazaar language was Dogri and Punjabi. The inability to speak the street language, while being perfectly understanding of all that was going on around, did not make my childhood strange or unique. At school, there were Punjabi children who understood Kashmiri but didn't speak it.

The sadhus who came to Kashmir in summer for pilgrimage and knocked at our gates for alms spoke Hindi in a variety of accents, and some spoke Tamil. We knew some European missionaries who spoke only English.

Kashmir is like the rest of India: less a melting-pot, more a living palimpsest. Each layer shows up astonishing oppositions. For example, after the Turks conquered Kashmir, it was decreed that Muslims will have pocket on the left side of the pheran for the Hindus had it on the right. These oppositions remind one of Jonathan Swift's Big-Endians and Little-Endians. In Lilliput such rivalry gave rise to six rebellions wherein one Emperor lost his life, and another his crown.

Life, those days, was spartan for father's salary as a veterinarian barely supported the family of seven, but it was rich culturally and emotionally and I don't recall any sense of deprivation. As children we viewed our lives in terms of duties, responsibilities, and doing well at school. Father was a good doctor and person, he had impeccable integrity, and he was not responsible for our difficult situation. Yes, he had a large family, but that was typical of those times.

We were raised on stories from the Mahābhārata, the Rāmāyana, the Purānas, and local folktales. Often the chowkidar in father's office came home in the evening for tea and as we huddled around he told us episodes from Kashmiri epics. One particularly gifted storyteller in Kulgam made remarkable embellishments to the tales to scare us. One evening when he had gone to bed, mother decided to pay him back in the same coin. She dressed up as a witch and, making strange sounds, began throwing rocks at his window. The poor guy was extremely frightened and believing it was a real witch he rushed out for help.

In small towns in India it is usual for employees to spend several hours in the evening after dinner, or on

Sundays during the day, at the supervisor's home, and this represents for them a pleasant departure from the humdrum routine of the day. Excepting the time mother took to make tea for the visitors, everyone, including the children was present in the living room. We had visitors practically every day, and the children, if not hearing folktales, were listening to office talk and commentaries on local and national politics.

The conversation often moved to the corruption in the bureaucracy. Father's own department was bad in this matter, and officers like father were expected to pay bribe to the clerk at the head office in Srinagar to get travel expenses approved and to get salary in time. There was no point complaining because the clerks shared the bribes with other staff and supervisors.

Sometimes, father's salary was stopped for months, which led to a lot of stress at home. Mother called father unworldly for not submitting to the demands of the clerks.

On a few occasions Babuji sent money from Kapurthala that helped forestall a difficult situation. More often we had to buy the groceries on credit.

What we saw of the workings of father's department made us quite certain that we did not want to work for the government. The corruption was worse in public works, police, and departments with greater revenue. Being naïve, we believed that such problems existed only in Kashmir and the rest of India was marching ahead.

5. Winter Ideas

Winters in Kashmir are long and cold. The season is traditionally divided into three periods of decreasing severity called *chilai kalan* (40 days), *chilai khorda* (20 days), and *chilai bacha* (10 days). The houses lacked insulation, and the only heating was from the kangri that also warmed the covers at night. This forced inactivity made it easy to get lost in one's own pursuits.

I asked father about meditation. He said all that was needed was the quieting of the mind, but this was easier said than done. The more one tried to force out thoughts they would come back. The mind is easily distracted which is why it is compared to a monkey.

It was much later I realized that meditation means letting go, which is easy but sometimes can be terrifying. I learnt to travel in space and time in mind's sky. Lying in bed, I would think of myself in the remote future when the solar system was dead, and I would get such an overpowering feeling of aloneness and emptiness that I would let out a scream.

In our homes, during the vacation months of mid-December to mid-March, we spent the day under layers of blankets. I had a seat on the matted floor with a small desk in front. I hardly stirred from the room, excepting perhaps to listen to the radio shows in the evening.

Apart from reading all I could, I was writing something or the other. When that bored me, I played with numbers and considered different ways to solve mathematical problems.

I was especially interested in prime numbers and searched for different kinds of number sequences with amusing properties. This was not hard to do. For example, if one multiplies 2, 3, and 5, the product of 30 is a sum of all the primes counted down from this number:

    23+7
    19+11
    17+13

As another example, consider the product of three non-consecutive primes 42=2×3×7. Here we have the following:

    37+5
    31+11
    29+13
    23+19

The situation is truly impressive for 210=2×3×5×7. This number is the sum of all the primes counted down from this number:

    199+11
    197+13
    193+17
    191+19
    181+29
    179+31
    173+37

167+43
163+47
157+53
151+59
149+61
139+71
137+73
131+79
127+83
113+97
109+101
107+103

Of course, this property holds up only partially for other multiples of primes. Numbers have other properties of symmetry and beauty and I whiled away hours playing with them.

I was also intrigued by Pythagorean triples that I was to use many years later for new encryption schemes. A Pythagorean triple (a, b, c) consists of positive integers that are the sides of a right triangle and thus $a^2 + b^2 = c^2$. I didn't know at that time that this theorem was known to Baudhāyana centuries earlier.

The areas (of the squares) produced separately by the length and the breadth of a rectangle together equal the area (of the square) produced by the diagonal. This theorem was used in India to measure off right-angled, triangulated distances in the building of altars. There is infinity of these triples such as:

3, 4, 5
12, 5, 13
15, 8, 17
7, 24, 25

I was intrigued by transformations between spaces and, in particular, I spent much time reading up on the theory of relativity and other topics of modern physics. Of course, I didn't really understand the deeper aspects of these subjects.

———

My childhood years belonged to a time much simpler than now. In small country schools of the state, we were taught history as story. We sat on mat and mostly did mathematical problems or the teacher just read from the textbook for the schools had no laboratories for science experiments.

In Udhampur, I was thrilled when I read the ringing declaration of Emperor Aśoka at the conclusion of his first rock edict:

esahi vidhi ya iyam:
dhammena palana, dhammena vidhane,
dhammena sukhiyana, dhamena gotiti

The word dhamma (or dharma) is usually translated as law although it could also mean tradition or truth. If we choose the common meaning, Aśoka's declaration becomes:

For this is my rule:
government by the law, of the law;
prosperity by the law, protection by the law.

Imagine my surprise when at high school I came across the similar-sounding concluding invocation in Lincoln's Gettysburg address: "government of the people, by the people, and for the people." Lincoln was echoing Daniel

Webster's 33-year old speech in the Senate where he spoke of the "people's government, made for the people, made by the people, and answerable to the people." But it is likely that both Webster and Lincoln had borrowed this phrase from John Wycliffe (14th century), the first translator of Latin Bible to English, who says in the prologue of the translation: "This Bible is for the Government of the People, by the People, and for the People."

This led to a puzzle: Was Aśoka's declaration the inspiration for Wycliffe (and Lincoln) through intermediary story-tellers who took the phrase from India to Europe, or was it just a coincidence?

We know of the transmission of stories westward from India as in the Pancatantra that was translated to Kalilah wa-Dimnahin Arabic (after the names of the two jackals Karataka and Damanaka). These stories and those from the Kathā-Sarita-Sāgara became part of the Arabian Nights and the Sindbad story-cycle. There are parallels between the Pancatantra and Aesop's fables. The name of the influential philosophical movement of Brethren of Purity (Ikhwan al-safa) is itself traced to one of the Pancatantra stories.

A European example of story transmission is the Christian legend of Barlaam and Josaphat. The legend tells how an Indian king persecutes his own son, Josaphat, who astrologers have foretold will establish the Christian Church. In due course, Josaphat meets the hermit Saint Barlaam and converts to Christianity. In the end, the prince's father accepts the son's conversion and retires to the desert to spend his last days with the old teacher. The legend became so popular in Europe that, from time to time, the Church announced that the relics of the two saints had appeared miraculously which were then installed with solemn ceremony. Barlaam and Josaphat were elevated to sainthood

55

by Georgian and Greek churches and found their way into the Roman Martyrology (27 November) and the Greek calendar (26 August).

Church scholars now acknowledge that Barlaam and Josaphat is a play on the names Bhagavān and Bodhisattva and a reworking of the story of Buddha's enlightenment. The original story was a Mahāyāna text that was translated into Arabic and European languages. Indeed this legend should not startle us for St. Ann, St. Lucy, St. Denis and St. Brigid, representing pre-Christian deities Anna, Lucia, Dionysus and Brighid, were similarly assimilated.

The echo of Indian stories in the early gospels and the influence of Vedanta and Buddhism on Gnosticism is also well accepted. In particular, the non-canonical Gospel of Thomas (which was discovered at Nag Hammadi in 1945) resonates with Indian ideas of spirituality.

Many scholars have given opinions on the possible relationship between the New Testament and Indian texts. The philosopher Arthur Schopenhauer (1788-1860) went so far as to suggest that the canonical gospels had an Indian basis: "The New Testament ... must be in some way traceable to an Indian source: its ethical system, its ascetic view of morality, its pessimism, and its Avatar, are all thoroughly Indian. It is its morality which places it in a position of such emphatic and essential antagonism to the Old Testament, so that the story of the Fall is the only possible point of connection between the two."

The Indologist Max Müller also spoke of the connections: "That there are startling coincidences between Buddhism and Christianity cannot be denied, and it must likewise be admitted that Buddhism existed at least 400 years before Christianity. I go even further, and should feel extremely grateful if anybody would point out to me the historical channels through which Buddhism had influenced early Christianity."

This challenge was met by Rudolf Seydel who showed that the originals of the events in the gospels are in the Lalitavistara Sūtra, and he listed fifty-one parallels. Some of these are: virginal conception by Mary and Maya, the annunciation by the angels, the star in the east, the tree that bends down to aid the mother, and the old sage who predicts the child's future. Further specific parallels are in Luke's infancy narrative, in the story of the good thief, the story of the temptation of Jesus, the prediction of his death as in John 12.34, or the story of the aged Simeon in Luke 2:25 (the Buddhist Asita), or the passage John 7:38.

Some see the parallels as no more than coincidences. If there was borrowing, it is hard to take the view that the Christian gospels were the source since the life stories of the Buddha were translated into Chinese from Sanskrit as early as the eleventh year of the reign of Emperor Ming of the Eastern Han Dynasty (69 CE), and this is much prior to the time the gospels were written down.

Recently the Danish Sanskrit scholar Christian Lindtner looked at the Greek versions of the gospels according to Matthew, Mark, Luke, and John and argued that much material in the gospels is a direct word-for-word, sentence-for-sentence translation of Buddhist material. He believes the original Sanskrit is from the Mūla-sarvāstivāda-vinaya (MSV) and the Saddharma-puṇḍarīka-sūtra (SDP), also known as the Lotus Sūtra. The complete text of MSV was translated only in recent years and therefore this constitutes important new evidentiary material.

Lindtner argues that the Christian trinitas (trinity) corresponds to the triratna of Buddhism, which crowns a flag standard on the frieze sculptures at Sanchi, which is couple of hundred years prior to the birth of Christianity. He further claims that puns, symbols, codes, and parables were translated into the gospels and there are obscure passages that only make sense in the Sanskrit original.

Yet the parallels or borrowings do not reduce the differences between the practice of Christianity and Buddhism. Even if Christianity borrowed Buddhist stories, they were put to a different use.

––––––––––

There are also interesting similarities in the service in the Church and the Buddhist temple. This was first noted by the French Lazarist missionaries, Evariste Huc and Joseph Gabet, who were amongst the first Westerners to visit Lhasa in 1840s. Their travels through Asia and Tibet were chronicled in Huc's book "Souvenirs d'un voyage dans la Tartarie, le Thibet et la Chine pendant les années 1844, 1845 et 1846." Huc listed the following similarities: "The cross, the miter, the dalmatica, the cope, ..., the service with double choirs, the psalmody, the exorcisms, the censer at suspended from five chains, the benedictions given by the Lamas by extending the right hand over the heads of the faithful, the chaplet, ecclesiastical celibacy, spiritual retirement, the worship of the saints, the fasts, the processions, the litanies, the holy water, all these are analogies between the Buddhists and ourselves."

Huc thought that the borrowing was by the Tibetans. But Tibetan Buddhism follows ancient prescriptions on ritual and worship, and it is implausible it copied the practices of a remote creed. It is more likely that the Tibetan and the Catholic rituals have a common source.

––––––––––

Nursery rhymes with nonsense words have also travelled. Consider:

58

Eenie, meenie, miney, moe/catch a tiger by the toe
If he hollers let him go/eenie, meenie, miney moe

This appears in English for the first time in the 19th century. In Germany, where it was known earlier, it has the form

Ene mene miste/Es rappelt in der Kiste
Ene mene meck/Und Du bist weg

Some claim that the original is the fifteen-hundred year old Sanskrit mantra (where words do not necessarily have meaning)

Ene mene dasphe/danda dasphe...

Of course, the English rhyme has also been copied in Hindi films as in

Ina mina dika/daye dame nika/maka naka naka and
akkara bakkar bambai bo/eena meena mo

Could *Hocus Pocus*, used as an exclamation by magicians, also have an Indian connection? According to some etymologists, it is a play on the sacramental blessing from the Mass, *Hoc est corpus meum* (this is my body); another theory derives it from the Latin *hicce es doctus* (here is the learned man). But there are exactly the same words in Kashmir, which are used as a magical formula. The Kashmiri rhyme begins with *hukus bukus:*

hukus bukus/teli wan che kus
onum batta lodum degi/
shaal kich kich waangano

Only the third line has a clear meaning which is "I got rice and put it in a pot." The rest is play on sounds.

Looking at the example of nonsense rhymes, it is plausible that the line from Aśoka's edict traveled to Europe and ended up in Abraham Lincoln's great speech.

6. DIFFERENT LENSES

I was growing up as the powerful effects of cinema and TV were bringing about rapid change in society. In the past, the power of the image was counterbalanced by the heard word, whose potential expands in tune with the inner beat. Now, mythology is largely banished or made into jumble of stories in schoolbooks and its connection with the domain of the spirit has been broken. We seemed to be imprisoned in the present as if by the mirror of Narcissus that freezes the capacity to go beyond the image.

Popular Hindi movies and film songs mapped the heightened emotionalism of post-independence politics into corresponding sentimentality in relationships. But more than this, the West loomed big in our imagination through its arts and ideas of history and change.

We read Herodotus, Xenophon, and Julius Caesar for history, and plays of Aeschylus, Euripides, and Sophocles for early literature, and also modern Western sages and philosophers. Their ideas superseded the Islamic division into *momin* and *kafir* that had framed Indian history for a thousand years.

Indian politics now began to mirror the dichotomy of Western thought. On the one side were those whose primary concern is the body: this is the camp of the left, and it includes socialists and communists and others who want experts to regulate society. On the other side was the right, which believes that the spirit should play a central role in polity and it includes traditionalists and the representatives of religion. If the left spoke of progress, the right spoke of thehuman spirit and tradition.

The left wishes man to go back to the natural state. It supports sexual freedom because that is what one sees in the animal kingdom, although some animals mate for life. The right believes that one's personal drives should be balanced with the demands of family and society.

Ever since revolutionary Paris of the 1790s, the left has sought to tear down social institutions and moral codes associated with tradition. Revolutionary France wished to destroy not only the monarchy and the nobility, but also organized religion and the family.

The left has adapted to historical conditions. With the rise of the Soviet Union, its main objective became socialist control. The West experimented with increased taxation and bureaucratic regulation. The adoption of sexual revolution as one of its goals by modern feminism is a hallmark of the post-socialist left. This was in opposition to the attitudes of most educated women until the sixties when magazines and books took men to be the initiators and beneficiaries of sexual liberation, and women as intolerant of promiscuity and victims of predatory men.

The introduction of the contraceptive pill around 1960 brought fundamental change. Fears of overpopulation legitimated a contraceptive ethic throughout middle-class society in the West and these ideas were quickly adopted by China, India and other countries. The pill gave women a feeling of control over sexual activity and eroded the social and psychological resistance to premarital sex. The West embraced no-fault divorce, first adopted by the Bolsheviks following the Russian Revolution of 1917. This began to undermine the idea of marriage as a binding mutual contract oriented toward the procreation and nurturing of children.

Early versions of feminism tended to embrace children and elevate motherhood, but the more recent adversarial feminism preaches that children and childbearing are the central instrumentality in the subjugation of women.

The political alliance of the left is based on group identity and encouraging feelings of victimhood. The left speaks of justice, whereas the right speaks of laws and contracts. Since there ought to be laws that provide justice and a perfect society does not exist, one needs a balance between the two positions.

The notion of the individual varies across cultures depending on the underlying cosmology, which is encapsulated as myth. In it are hidden thought patterns by which the community approaches its place in the universe, attains self-knowledge and self-confidence, defines its place in an ecological sense, and formulates its destiny.

The difference in behavior amongst different cultures is not based on difference in rationality (as assumed by some anthropologists) but on the difference in constructed reality. Commonsense is logical behavior in the reality created by the mind, and if this reality is different for different individuals, one may mistakenly assume that the individuals were using different logic to interpret the same reality.

The notion of the individual is also tied up with eschatology, which is the theological doctrine of the end of the world. The theories of the individual and grand narratives on the end of the world have a bearing on behavior, explaining difference in social organization.

Jews, Christians, and Muslims share a belief in a final cataclysm and the appearance of a messianic redeemer. Part of the intractability of the conflict in Israel is that each side is reading its own eschatology in the unfolding events. For some Christians, there is:

- The second coming of Jesus Christ, when he returns to earth after almost two millennia.
- The war of Armageddon -- a massive battle in Israel.
- The arrival on earth of the Antichrist, an evil political, military leader.
- The Tribulation, a seven year interval of great suffering and death.
- The Rapture, when Christians who have been born again -- both living and dead -- will rise into the sky towards Jesus.

It was the expectation of this second coming that caused many to fear the onset of the new millennium. In order to forestall panic withdrawal from banks, the US printed a lot of extra money which, in turn, added to the Information Technology bubble and its subsequent crash. The stimulus to lessen the effects of the bursting of this bubble by encouraging investment in housing led, in turn, to the 2008 crash.

For the Muslims, the coming of the Mahdi is accompanied by minor signs, such as: wine drinking, love of this world, hatred of death, neglect of prayer, interest on loans, and popularity of singing women. The major signs include the emergence of the Deceiver (Al-Dajjal), who is the equivalent of the Christian Antichrist. Amongst the followers of the Deceiver will be seventy thousand Jews of Isfahan wearing Persian shawls. The Dajjal is not only an incarnation of evil in the guise of a global leader, but can also be a system of social and cultural phenomena, as well as an unseen power. Some say that Western democracy could qualify as the Great Deceiver. Another major sign is that the sun will rise in the west.

The Last Hour would not come unless the Muslims fight against the Jews and kill them and the Jews hide behind a stone or a tree, and the stone or the tree says: Muslim, or the servant of Allah, there is a Jew behind me; come and kill him (Hadith Abu-Harayah in Book 40, Number 6985). In the mind of the pious Muslim, the ongoing reforestation in Israel is a defensive maneuver by the Jews to delay the Day of Judgment.

The struggle between the West and the Islamic world is, for the true believers on both sides, a religious struggle. My Muslim friends were vaguely aware of this opposition. They were clearer of the opposition to the Hindus that in banter is expressed as Islamic equality versus Hindu hierarchy. This is symbolized by the *trāma* at the Muslim wedding, which is the dinner plate shared by four people who sit around it.

7. AMERICA AND INDIA

America entered my consciousness first through the photographs of the construction workers on the unfinished floors of a skyscraper — looking fearless, laughing at the frozen traffic of the street fifty-odd floors below — in an old encyclopedia at home. I went over this volume again and again, and with each new visit the subjects of the photographs appeared bigger, until America became a mythic presence.

Later in the high school in Leh, I saw illustrated books that described early English colonies in Massachusetts and Virginia. The encounter between the scantily-clad natives and the English in their gleaming red uniforms seemed to bridge a stark opposition.

Political news passed for entertainment in those days, and the binary polarity of capitalism versus communism, with America and Russia as the respective leaders, was always on our mind. If United States was liked for its religious liberty, Russia was praised for creating a society of equals (as informed by newspaper propaganda). If the West was criticized for its association with colonialism, Russia was criticized for lack of freedom.

In those times, smart young Muslims were attracted to communism for this was a way to an imagined perfect state without the religiosity of the Islamic utopia. When communism as ideology collapsed, young Muslims felt their only option was to work for the return of the Caliphate.

This was the time that burqa was common as part of the formal attire for Muslims in small towns and villages. When women worked in the fields, they did not wear burqa.

Of the many forms of the sacred, those of total abandonment and total concealment are the most powerful — more than the skirt of the minister and the mullah, or the ashes and the saffron shawl of the swami. I didn't know this in the Kashmir of my boyhood for it was then a place of sober moderation where people went through their ritual out of habit, without passion. Propriety counted for everything. The breast-beating of Muharram was a gentlemanly affair. I was to see the bloody frenzy with knives and chains much later in Ladakh.

The burqa of the women in the bazaar was a common vanity, but it covered only partially, without sanctimony. These were poor people who wore their piety to show off that they were more religious than they actually were to strangers, to earn anonymity from people who did not care for them.

We were innocent then, building our worlds out of the fragments of old habit. A distant relative lost his job soon after he was married. Every morning he left home — he and his wife lived with his parents — with a packed lunch and briefcase and took the bus to a park, where he spent the entire day. Relatives knew his situation, but he carried on with the charade because he did not wish his wife to know, for fear of losing face. She actually knew, but pretended otherwise. This went on for several weeks, fooling no one but strangers on the bus and the bazaar.

An evil wind destroyed that old Kashmir. I had a premonition of this disaster on a visit thirty years ago in the averted eyes, in the barely concealed rage in people I knew. It was a rage unlike the one that sprouts from a personal wrong. It was like a fog that hung over the place in heavy layers, covering everyone, even those who would normally be happy in their own world.

That's when I saw the total shroud. It was not the badge of poverty of the burqa of my childhood, but a covering that hid everything excepting the eyes — a sign of nameless passion by stylish women who wished to be the usherettes of a terrible, retributive revolution. They were not like the women I had grown up with, nor those I had seen in the Middle Eastern airports who threw off their veil the moment the plane took off beyond the reach of the moral police.

The total shroud may appear similar to the mask, but isn't. The mask arouses temptation; it makes the reveler anonymous, as it did in the masquerade balls of the carnival. In times long past the Church opposed masks, fearing they tampered with human appearance and invited idolatry, disingenuousness, and the devil. The shroud separates the worlds of men and women, to limit possibilities here so that one may dream of paradise — there can be no arrival or transformation, only rage, dislocation, wistfulness.

Kashmiris have adjusted to the taboos of music, dance or song by cloaking it in religious garb. Religious hardliners, who disavow the arts, refuse to see things for what they are as if by agnosia caused by injury to the brain. The sensitive amongst them deny their experience and even falsify things and history, only revealing them, through hints beyond conventional forms and words, by an excessive sentimentality and repetitive motions.

America, in spite of its vast spaces, lacks the sancties that spring from the magic of childhood not merely one's own, but also of forefathers. Even more, America remains the region of worldly contest. Now that after 911 war has come to the shores of America, its certitudes appear naïve, and the contest has lost its excitement.

It is a common conceit to think that one's own way is the only correct one. Other cultures see their place in the universe in manner different from ours. Even within the same nation, people with different religious faith or those in different stages of life relate to life in uniquely different ways. From this perspective, there is no single reality.

Through the binary of two cultures in Kashmir, one ancient of which we were a part and to which we were joined by remembrance of events and places, the other revolutionary, seeking to destroy all that did not agree with its beliefs, we came to see how the same reality takes different shapes in the minds of different people.

This multiple reality drives history at the personal level and at the levels of community and nation. Those who believe that there is no correct vision but their own want others to say they are seeing the same which leads to political and religious wars.

Scientific and moral laws have specific ranges of applicability. Beyond that, between physical reality and the experiencing self lies the agency of the mind. This middle space involves the subject and, therefore, it can only be addressed by philosophy – where words stretch to provide insight that cannot be reduced to simple declarations.

Although metaphysics deals with existence and reality, its formal study is limited to narratives on reality and existence. The study of knowledge and ethics are also mutually dependent and related to politics and aesthetics, which are choices in the field of force and power and the sense of art and life. But due to the limitations of language, these conceptions are shadows whose original form remains elusive.

Language expresses associations between things in a sequential manner, whereas their unfolding is simultaneous and parallel. Nevertheless, language provides the infrastructure with which we construct our ordinary view of reality and even if this view is limited, analysis of meaning can help obtain important and deep insight. In particular, such analysis makes one aware of paradoxes that inform us of the limitations of our knowledge.

The beginning cannot be unitary, because the one cannot, by itself, become many, and it can only be defined in relation to others. There can neither be only one, nor many at the beginning, because that would undermine order, and imply perennial chaos. The beginning must thus not be of things, but of the order itself, together with the potential for all its manifestations.

When manifestations reside as impressions they become the ground on which further expressions of the unfolding takes place. When viewed in the mind's eye, one becomes aware of duality which is the sense of the other and its multiplicity. Out of this sense come counting and mathematics.

Body and mind are not identical. The self is the bridge that spans many layers of being. Since the body is the base on which the mind rests, its examination can reveal subtle layers of experience. The interrelationships in the outside world, in the physical world as well as in society, are mirrored in the organization of the body.

Metaphysics cannot be reduced to logic: it deals with paradox and inversion. Art and creative action illustrates this most clearly. Time flies into the future, but we live facing the past, and so are burdened by it. What we seek in search of happiness is precisely what is sure to bring despair. Although we speak of the world as a collection of things, we can only celebrate impermanence.

In the sixties, we didn't know all this about recursion, concealment and pursuit of power. Since experience teaches one to seek out the middle path, we did not understand why, in spite of its professed commitment to liberty, the United States chose to aid and support some of the worst dictators in the world.

The newspapers told us that America did so since communism was a one-way street. The free world could not, therefore, afford to let even one additional country move over to the communist camp.

Very few Indians had then been to the United States and experienced life there. The real power of America lay in its books and movies. Russia had produced great novelists in the nineteenth century but the communist era had been one long drought. Boris Pasternak and Alexander Solzhenitsyn were major writers but their art was about the tragedy of lost freedoms in the communist system. This was the time Western writers were producing influential novels and academic tomes dealing with all kinds of human problems and concerns.

Sergei Eisenstein may have been a pioneer in films, but the world watched Hollywood. If American movies were not shown, their ideas arrived there sooner or later through copies made by Hindi film directors.

The declared Indian political policy was of nonalignment with both the communists and the capitalistsbut we knew that the muddled socialism of the government could only be a passing phase and eventually the economy will be based on more rational ground.

The Indian mind is particularly attracted to abstractions. This explains the enduring fascination for ideology of all kind, such as sadhus who live their life devoted to a vow, social communities that choose to wear only white, or still others that wear no clothes. Even religious devotion — bhakti — is sometimes taken to the extreme. To counter extreme sentimentality, Indian sages exhorted people to follow the middle path.

In the fifties, we seemed to have lost the sense of that middle way. Perhaps the elite believed that the country was not ready for democracy for India was ruined by the century-and-a-half of British rule, the level of poverty was unimaginable, and for most the only security was to be had in a government job. In this system, ministers and bureaucrats came to wield immense power.

The government claimed to be non-aligned with both of the two great powers of the post-War years. But it was seen as being more on the side of the Soviets in the international rivalries of the day. Within India, we saw this rivalry through many prisms. People were grateful to the Soviet Union for bailing India out by exercising its veto in the Security Council, but they did not like communist totalitarianism. On the other side, there was dismay with the level of poverty of African-Americans in the United States.

Indian states mimicked the government sponsored personality cults of the communist countries. At the top of the pyramid, we lived in the constant company of Jawaharlal Nehru. He was everywhere: in the newspapers and on the radio. The school textbooks had chapters on him and his family and he strode the stage of world politics like a giant. But in the evenings when we would discuss the world scene over dinner we would often wonder if he wasn't Don Quixote rather than modern-day Emperor Aśoka.

We were convinced that he was a brilliant man, but wondered why he had failed to counter Pakistan's bellicosity. If his non-aligned movement was such a great idea, why were its members some of the worst-run countries? If he had found a new way to progress why wasn't it appreciated elsewhere in the world; and why were we still poor? It felt as if India had entered mythic time in which we were part of a national theater celebrating the socialist paradise with Nehru as prophet, and it didn't matter if this paradise was out of joint with reality.

The Nehru years were a period of public celebration and private fears. We congratulated each other in public discourse, repeating platitudes about the moral superiority of the non-aligned nations of which India was the leader. Our achievements were measured by the brilliance of our rhetoric; we were especially proud of the nine-hour speech at the United Nations by ambassador Krishna Menon. Although certain that Nehru's path of license-raj was wrong for the country, we were so mesmerized by his energy and style and his mastery of the political vocabulary.

How did Nehru seize the public imagination in India so well? He was a complex man, with drive and self-discipline and an insatiable thirst for power. He was prone to dark moods and he had an ugly temper, but he was also sophisticated and well-read with interests in science and technology. He was a clever politician and also a genuine leader who was much loved and admired.

He was a good writer, because he had the capacity to reflect on his actions and question people like Gandhi on occasion. He gave long sanctimonious speeches that left his opponents frustrated. Nehru's idea of non-aligned nations made him a star in Africa and Asia, but the Americans and the Europeans saw him as a tool of the Russians. People with historical insight saw him as a well-intentioned person driven by idealism who was somewhat out of touch with the realities of power.

He sought an international role for India much in excess of its economic and military power. The injection of morality into the discourse of international relations, showed inexperience in geopolitical affairs and his reputation suffered greatly when, in spite of slogans of *Hindi-Chini Bhai-Bhai*, the Chinese turned on him in the late fifties. Nehru had little administrative experience and he was blinded by Lenin's example and by the theories of British socialists. The economic course on which he placed India after independence set the country back by a half-century.

In spite of the impressionable years spent in England, Nehru was very Indian in his belief system. He had faith in a special destiny that is quite common in our land of avatars and rishis, gurus and reformers, world-conquerors and wise sages. This faith is reinforced by the expectations of the public that their leaders be heroic. Ancient Indian political theory speaks of the king who spends several years in the wilderness and then returns to claim the crown.

Gandhi was such a hero who had appeared as superhuman in his political and personal struggles in South Africa and later in India. By his example, he was able to inspire others into actions of which they could have hardly believed they were capable.

As Gandhi's chief political heir, Nehru sought great challenges and he tried to build a hodge-podge socialist state with a "human face." The Indian system remained imperial during his administration; in fact, he added layers of bureaucratic control inspired by the Soviet example. He vacillated and made grand gestures. The ambivalence that he engendered made him appealing and powerful.

When he was alive the intellectuals in India applauded his policies, but since the government controlled the media, discordant voices were not heard. Corruption scandals engulfed some of his associates but Nehru appeared disengaged. The great blow to his mythic persona was the Chinese invasion of 1962 that forced him to seek American aid.

Nehru's Congress Party ruled India continuously since independence for fifty years, excepting for a small interregnum of three years. Its ideology was socialist but its approach was a confused mixture of the policies of Western European democracies and the Soviet Union. In actual practice, the government operated by the license-quota Raj, in which the smallest initiative required license by the government and different communities were guaranteed a certain proportion of government jobs.

This system, which was designed to exercise patronage and control, was perfect for corruption. If the state did not collapse, it was because there were many upright individuals and politicians who kept the system running. The late eighties and the nineties saw the rise of a powerful new movement seeking regeneration and authenticity. However, it was focused primarily on symbols and leaders did not quite know what was to be done by way of actual change.

8. Naseem Bagh

I was fifteen when I joined engineering college in Naseem Bagh in 1962. This college was established a couple of years earlier in makeshift barracks under the chinar trees of a Mughal garden facing the Dal Lake. It sat next to the town of Hazratbal, an ancient pilgrimage center that is now an important Muslim shrine in the valley. Naseem Bagh was its temporarylocationand the permanent campus was to be built on the other side of Hazratbal. Its small library was better than any I had seen, and it had a recent edition of the Encyclopedia Britannica.

I was just out of high school when mother pushed me to apply to the college. Those days the two chief career options were engineering and medicine and I had foreclosed the latter option by not taking biology at college.

I had high rank in the statewide examination and was called for the interview where I was told that I was too young for the program. But several weeks later, I received the letter of admission as a result of a complaint aired in personal audience with President S. Radhakrishnan by a student who, like me, had been denied admission. The President called for an investigation and it turned out that many Kashmiri Hindu students with high rank had been unjustly rejected. Now, a new batch of students was let in and we were housed in big open halls of wooden barracks. When asked to choose the area of specialization, I picked electrical engineering only because Avinash was doing that in Madras.

The living accommodations were rudimentary. Initially, several dozens of us were housed in the same barrack with the toilet facilities in a separate shed. Both sides of the barrack were lined with beds, alternating with a chair, a small table with a table lamp atop. A few months later, after some additional construction had been completed, I, like others, was assigned to a five-student room and this continued until we graduated. There was no personal space in such an arrangement and one had to go to the library or sit under a tree to read. Beyond the perimeter of the college was a tea shop.

Some of my teachers were quite good; a few of them had Ph.D. They were reasonably effective at teaching basic applied mathematics of the engineering courses. The college was residential and about half the student body was from outside the state.

Soon after, the Chinese-India war began. On October 20, 1962, China attacked south of the Karakoram Pass at an end of the Aksai Chin Plateau and in the Pangong Lake area. The defending Indian forces lost several posts but they put up spirited resistance at the key posts of Daulat Beg Oldi and Chushul (located immediately south of Pangong Lake and at the head of the vital supply road to Leh). In the eastern sector, in Assam, the Chinese forces advanced relatively easily. By November 18, they had penetrated close to the outskirts of Tezpur, a major frontier town. They did not advance farther, declaring unilateral cease-fire on November 21. By the time the fighting stopped, each side had lost about 500 troops, and Jawaharlal Nehru's prestige had suffered a grievous blow.

In late December 1963, a hair from the beard of the prophet Muhammad was stolen from the reliquary at the Hazratbal

Mosque in Srinagar. As the news of the theft spread, huge crowds from all over Kashmir began to converge to Hazratbal in spite of bitter cold and heavy snowfall. People were disconsolate and they wept and wailed that now they will not see the blessed relic.

After several weeks, there was a report that the hair was recovered and the caretaker had been arrested. The crowds remained skeptical and insisted on proof, and the situation got more dangerous by the day. In Anantnag, from the window of our apartment near the Bus Station, we could see menacing crowds from the villages congregate and board buses for Hazratbal. The shops were shut down for days and the fear was that we will be victims of uncontrollable violence.

Nehru sent his trusted deputy, Lal Bahadur Shastri, to negotiate with the activists. He was able to persuade that in such a situation the best course was a *deedar* (showing) to convince it was the genuine article.

The *deedar* was arranged and at the appointed time, in front of a huge throng, a respected Muslim leader examined the relic. He held it for a full minute and then spoke out in clear voice that it indeed was genuine. There were cheers and the worst had been averted. But the activists held on and began to agitate for punishment to the criminals responsible for the theft.

The matter of who had stolen the relic was a sensitive one. It was rumored that it had been removed for private showing for a sick lady from a powerful Kashmiri family. The government held on to the story that it had mysteriously reappeared and they had no further information.

This went on for several weeks. The shops remained closed and business was hurting badly. The government and the opposition now came up with a face-saving formula. The police smashed the padlocks of the shops, giving the shopkeepers a reason to come back and resume business. I was witness to the breaking of the padlocks in street after street in Anantnag.

———

Jawaharlal Nehru had developed a strategic partnership with the Soviet Union, which took India's side in the debates of the Security Council of the UN. The Soviet government directed the Indian communists to assume a supportive role towards the Congress governments.

Meanwhile, the relations between the governments of the Soviet Union and China soured. In the early 1960s, the Communist Party of China began criticizing the CPSU of turning revisionist and deviating from the path of Marxism–Leninism. Sino-Indian relations also deteriorated leading to the war of 1962.

During this war, one faction of the Indian communists backed the Indian government while another faction took China's side. The China-supporting party came to be called CPI (Marxist) or simply CPM. Hundreds of Communist Party leaders, who were pro-Chinese, were imprisoned. In 1964, the pro-China delegates held a convention in Tenali that was marked by the display of a large portrait of the Chinese Communist leader Mao Zedong.

The CPM followed the Trotskyite template of "transitional demand" that whips people to continually agitate for unattainable goals to keep them angry so that additional cracks appear in the system that will eventually make political victory possible. To this end, they formed alliances with the most regressive political and religious groups in which each side thinks that the other side is idiotic but must be taken advantage of for the larger goal.

When in power, the CPM used instruments of the state for the patronage of its cadre and police repression on the opponents. Its polity was backward looking driven by appeal to envy and resentment in the pursuit of absolute power.

———

I remember the monster snowstorm of 1964. It came on the night of tenth December when we had just finished our examinations. The next day all road traffic came to halt and electric power failed. The skies now cleared, the temperature fell below -10 degrees Celsius, and the accumulated snow began to freeze.

We were stranded in Hazratbal. The freeze over the Dal Lake in front of the college expanded. On the fourteenth, my friend Som Nath Pandit and I walked ten miles on the icy roads to Srinagar to inquire when the bus service will resume, and knocked at the place of my aunt (Chand Rani) on the Bund where she made us a hot meal on the kerosene stove. We trudged back to the college by nightfall.

Next morning, we walked back to Srinagar and I got a seat in the first bus after the storm to leave for Anantnag. This bus started at 4:30 PM but took over four hours to do the thirty-six miles. Along the way we had to get down several times to clear the road of the frozen snow. After I reached Anantnag, I came down with a bad fever.

———

Nehru died in May 1964. Lal Bahadur Shastri, who had handled the Hazratbal crisis well, succeeded him as prime minister. Pakistan tested him in the Rann of Kutch dispute in 1965 and felt he had been weak-kneed. Believing that Indian military had not recovered from its loss to China, the Pakistani president Ayub Khan went along the hawks in his cabinet, who were led by Zulfikar Ali Bhutto, to attack Kashmir.

On August 5, 1965 over 30,000 Pakistani soldiers crossed the border dressed as Kashmiri locals. The Indians responded, and we heard fighter planes screech overhead and saw convoys of military trucks on the highway.

The initial battles, contained within Kashmir, involved both infantry and armor supported by air force. In early September, Pakistani forces attacked Akhnur in Jammu to choke Indian supply line to Kashmir and India countered by attacking targets within Pakistani Punjab, which forced the Pakistanis to disengage from Akhnur. There was a large but indecisive engagement in the Sialkot region where some 500 tanks squared off.

By September 22 both sides had agreed to a UN mandated cease-fire ending the war that had become largely a stalemate although India held somewhat larger territory. Pakistanis, raised on the propaganda of hate and martial prowess, as in the equation that one Pakistani was equal to four Indians, were shocked that their country had come close to military defeat. They blamed the failure on the ineptitude of Ayub Khan.

China gave political support to Pakistan during the war. The Soviet Union, rather than rallying reflexively to India's side, adopted a neutral position and ultimately provided its offices for talks at Tashkent, which led to the January 1966 Declaration that restored the status quo ante. Ayub Khan spoke now of the "triangular tightrope" of maintaining good ties with the United States while cultivating China and the Soviet Union.

The 1965 War brought to the open the ambivalence Kashmiri Muslims felt for the prevailing political arrangement. Kashmir's most popular politician, Sheikh Abdullah (1905-1982), was in jail. His political career was launched with an agitation for reforms in 1931 during the rule of Maharaja Hari Singh. Next year a political party, the Muslim Conference, was formed with Abdullah as its president. Under pressure from the British, the Maharaja set up a commission to suggest constitutional reforms that led to the establishment of a legislative assembly of seventy five members, thirty three of whom would be elected on a communal basis. When first convened in 1934, 19 of the 21 seats allotted to the Muslims were won by the Muslim Conference.

Sheikh Abdullah was much influenced by Jawaharlal Nehru, whom he first met in 1937. Having by now recognized that popular Islam represented his natural constituency, he enlarged the scope of his political party, renaming it the National Conference. His closeness to the Congress Party motivated the revival of the Muslim Conference by his opponents in Jammu who saw a convergence of their interests with the Muslims of the Punjab. His opponents felt that Sheikh Abdullah was endeavoring to define a special position for the Kashmiri Muslims.

At the national level, the sectarian Muslim League represented the aspirations of the orthodox Islamic minority of the mullahs, the Islamic intellectuals, and the descendants of immigrants from Central Asia and Iran. These groups felt that their apartness needed political guarantees that might not be otherwise available in democratic India.

———

At the time of the partition of India, the Muslim Conference, based mainly in Jammu, was in favor of the state's accession to Pakistan. The Maharaja was hoping to remain independent. There were other groups who wanted accession to India. Sheikh Abdullah and his National Conference also appeared to be working for independence but given a choice between Pakistan and India they felt that autonomy for Kashmir within the secular Indian Union was more desirable. The attack by the Pakistanis forced the hand of the Maharaja, and as the attackers reached the outskirts of Srinagar, the Maharaja sought the aid of the Indian army. He was asked to sign the formal Instrument of Accession which was done on 26 October 1947.

The next day, Indian troops flew in to protect Srinagar and soon the Pakistanis were in retreat. In three weeks, most of the Vale was in the control of the Indian army. The fighting reached a stalemate during the winter and Nehru referred the Kashmir dispute to the United Nations.

Meanwhile the war dragged on at other fronts. Pakistan tried to cut off Ladakh from Kashmir but did not succeed. In the autumn, the Indian army captured Poonch in the Jammu province. The Indian army now threatened to cut the Pakistan controlled area in two by reaching the international border beyond Poonch. There was pressure on both countries to stop fighting and cease-fire took effect on 1 January 1949.

In March 1948, Sheikh Abdullah was appointed the prime minister of the interim government of the state. A Constituent Assembly was convened in October 1951. In 1952, Jawaharlal Nehru and Sheikh Abdullah signed an agreement that specified that the state, while part of the Indian Union, enjoyed certain unique rights related to land ownership within the state. This fact was recognized in Article 370 of the Indian Constitution which was entitled "Temporary provisions with respect to the State of Jammu and Kashmir."

Sheikh Abdullah now began to implement a program that was outlined by the National Conference in 1944 in a manifesto entitled New Kashmir. This amounted to a one-party government dedicated to social reform in the style of the Soviet Union. Sheikh Abdullah's goal appeared to be autonomy for the Kashmiris, but he was unwilling to allow real democracy to the other regions of Jammu and Ladakh. Growing tensions in the State led to his dismissal and detention in August 1953. He was succeeded as prime minister by Bakshi Ghulam Mohammed who remained in power for 10 years.

The new constitution came into operation in January 1957. It delimited the constituencies to perpetuate control by the Kashmiris of the Vale. A policy of reservation in schools, colleges, and government jobs was instituted. These quotas applied not only at the entrance levels of the government departments but also for promotion to higher ranks. All citizens of the state excepting Kashmiri Hindus were declared backward and deserving of special favors in admission to schools and in government jobs.

When father received an attractive offer from Himachal Pradesh government, he was not given the *no-objection certificate* without which he could not join the new position.

9. Completing College

As student I read a lot, played sports and, in summer, swam in the Dal Lake. The college had a literary magazine for which I wrote from time to time. In August 1965, I stood first in an essay competition organized by Radio Kashmir. As a result I got to read the essay on the radio and was paid an honorarium. The college now selected me to write a play for a national University Drama Competition, and I wrote a historical play set in Kashmir, but never heard what came of it.

During the first winter holidays I went to Faridabad, near Delhi, to spend several weeks with my uncle Babuji, who was then the principal of a local college. To keep myself busy I brought with me several books of Greek and medieval English plays and a notebook in which I wrote poetry.

I quickly became a celebrity in the college in my first year when I won the general knowledge quiz that was open to all students of the college, which Moonis Raza, the new dean of students, had organized. I was to win this competition in subsequent years as well. Moonis Raza's own field was geography and he had been a student leader of the left at Aligarh Muslim University. He was an excellent conversationalist with an open and friendly disposition.

There was not much to do after the classes excepting sports and other games. Of cricket, badminton, and table tennis that I played, I was best at table tennis, becoming one of the college's strongest players. I also played a lot of chess, checkers, and carrom. In chess, I won the college and the university tournaments and represented Kashmir University in India's first inter-university chess tournament that was held in Srinagar.

My experience with the bureaucratic culture of the college was not so pleasant. It was common for professors to hold court like ministers or officers in government departments. Moonis Raza, who was meanwhile promoted to principal, held informal court for those who aspired to be leaders of student organizations. This style served to build bridges with the students, and to make the student feel that he was somehow a part of the professor's larger family. Such courts remain part of the bureaucratic culture of India, but I concluded that this style did not suit me.

Very early at the college I had an unpleasant experience on the cricket field. I challenged a senior student, who was a bully, when he kept on bowling after the end of his turn. He struck me and although I was right no one on the field spoke up for me. I left the field, my mouth bleeding, helpless about the matter.

I spent days and weeks reflecting on the individual's obligations in the face of violence and power. I was to experience this situation again when I was physically assaulted by a mathematics lecturer for laughing in his class. This time there was an inquiry and the lecturer left the college.

The classwork was easy enough. I realized that paying attention in the classroom was sufficient to do well at examinations, and there was no need to buy textbooks.

———

In 1966, there was a serious drought in Bihar and we collected money for the Relief Fund. Later that year, there was an agitation regarding some matter and the students went in a procession to a large meeting in the Dining Hall of the New Campus of the College and I was pushed up to stand on a table to give a speech.

The same year, Avinash spent the summer teaching at the college. After a brilliant record in the engineering program in Madras, he had been admitted to do Ph.D. at IIT Delhi. He had the summer off because the Ph.D. class did not start until August. During this period, we were part of two memorable hikes in the mountains: one to Kaunsarnag Lake at 12,000 feet via the Aharbal Falls, and another to Gangabal Lake of similar elevation at the foot of Mount Haramukh. These trips made several elements of the geography of Rājataraṅginī come alive.

An incident with enormous impact on me occurred later that year in winter. We were at the Bombay Zoo, a stop on an across-the-country college trip, and I was observing a pair of bears in their cage when my eyes met theirs and I experienced an overpowering feeling of mutual recognition. As I was reflecting on this feeling, the bears suddenly turned violent and started striking each other in apparent rage and soon they were bleeding from many cuts. It appeared as if the bears had put up the show to amuse me, to teach how it all was a game. I felt that my awareness was no different from that of them, although I was in the human body.

At one level I was an animal, no different from others, but I was an animal with special knowledge. The perception was ego shattering, but it seemed to expand my consciousness.

The experience hung about me for months. I felt that consciousness was universal, and this appeared to give me a sense of unique insight. I was able to get out of my skin and empathize with almost anyone, and there arose a sense of love that I wished to share with others. I also felt a strong emotion regarding mortality, for getting out of the body is akin to death.

Our final exams were held in July and at the end of it the only thing remaining was the thesis, to complete which we were granted a few more weeks. Over the years I had, on my own, read advanced physics and learnt its mathematical formalism. I was encouraged to write the thesis on quantum electrodynamics by my advisor, who was the head of the mathematics department and an expert on the subject. But, to be honest, it was more of playing with equations than any deep understanding of the subject.

In the meanwhile, in August, the Kashmiri Hindu community became agitated when a poor girl who was legally a minor eloped with a Muslim. The leaders of the community argued that the girl should be returned to her family. But this was not easily done since the Muslim community claimed that she had willingly embraced Islam and, therefore, sharia law should hold. The government had to tiptoe around the complexities of the case.

The case made the resentments regarding laws that discriminated in jobs and school and college admissions boil over. Every evening, people assembled and there were speeches by activists and housewives. This agitation went on for several weeks and some young people were killed in police firing.

During the early part of this period I came home to Srinagar often and saw much of the agitation. Mother and my sisters participated in processions and other demonstrations. I also found that my mother was quite fearless. One evening a young man, who was a youth leader, rushed into our home in the evening. A group of policemen arrived a bit later, knocked at the door, asking for the young man. Mother told them firmly that no outsider had entered the house.

In September, father was transferred to Jammu and over the next couple of months the paperwork for school transfer of my siblings had to be completed. The government was afraid that Kashmiri Hindus would leave the State in large numbers, so it made it difficult for their children to change their examination site. As my parents and siblings were already in Jammu, father asked me to get the form in Srinagar and sign for Jaishree for change of her exam to Jammu.

The bus in winter took nearly twelve hours to complete this journey. On this occasion the bus was stopped at Banihal, before the tunnel that takes one across the mountain to the valley, as the road to Srinagar was blocked by a snowstorm. The passengers had to spend the night in the hall of one of the ramshackle hotels in town. Those were the days when Kashmiris travelled with bedding in holdall and since I had no baggage I was in danger of freezing at night.

I sat at a corner of the hall not knowing what to do when a Kashmiri merchant, travelling with family who had spread the beddings on the floor, called me and said that I could lie down with his very young daughter who had a holdall-bed to herself. That surely saved me that night.

I went to see the vice-principal of the Women's College who had to sign off on Jaishree's form. This gentleman was the next door neighbor of my uncle Radha Krishen's where I was staying. But he refused to approve saying that the form required the presence of the student applicant.

Next day, I took the bus to Jammu and by the time we reached Qazigund before Verinag, the traffic came to halt and we were told that the convoy will proceed through the tunnel only the next day. This time a shopkeeper let me sleep in his shop in bedding he provided.

After reaching Jammu, Jaishree and I got into the bus for Srinagar. The weather had improved and there was no untoward incident. She got her approval and we returned to Jammu.

The Kashmir Hindu agitation was still going on although the winter had made it difficult to hold demonstrations. Now the government bought off some leaders and announced that the demands of the agitators will be met, and the movement was officially shut down. In reality nothing was conceded and people were ready to forget the agitation and move on with their lives.

I found out my results in late November: I had secured high marks in the final year. Now was the wait for the official certificates that took a few weeks. I spent this time with parents in Jammu at the Belicharana Farm where father was manager.

I received the official certificate on 18th December. That night I left for Delhi and joined the Ph.D. program at IIT the next day.

10. INFORMATION AND COMPUTERS

When I presented myself to Professor P.V. Indiresan, he directed me to Mahendra Singh Sodha of the physics department. Sodha's area of research was plasmas and he led a huge group, which was prolific at publishing. He had done a stint as post-doc at the University of British Columbia and worked for industry in the US before returning to India. His students were interested in mitigating the problem of the reentry blackout of spacecraft. The origin of the blackout was the envelope of ionized air created by the heat from the compression of the atmosphere by the craft. The idea was that a more accurate representation of the plasma around the craft will help develop methods to overcome the problem.

I wasn't sure that this problem was likely to have a solution, so I told Professor Indiresan that I preferred to work with him. He said that digital communication was to be my area of research. Avinash was also working under him.

Indiresan went on to become prominent in Indian scientific world. He established a laboratory in IIT Delhi for advanced research in electronics that did important work for Indian military. Later he became director of Indian Institute of Technology Madras, and next the president of Indian National Academy of Engineering.

Indiresan was short and wiry but a forceful personality. His interests were mainly in the applications of digital signal processing, while we brothers were interested in more fundamental research. He was broad-minded enough to let us work on whatever caught our fancy: Avinash chose to write his dissertation on electromagnetics and antennas, whereas I decided to work on the foundations of information theory.

The question of what constituted information had interested me for some time. In Srinagar, I had thought of it in terms of information that observers in motion may obtain about their perceived world, and this is what I spoke about in my admission interview. The interviewing committee thought my ideas were novel enough to merit direct admission into the program.

These were tough days for India. The summers were unusually hot and there were droughts in 1968 and 1969 with food shortage that was felt even in the dining halls of IIT. The government bought U.S. wheat at concessional rate under the Food for Peace program (PL-480), but this program had worsened India's agriculture productivity problem. The program sold the surplus production of the American farmer (some of which was bad) and alleviated hunger, but by disrupting market forces it had serious unintended consequences.

During the worst days of the drought, each chapāti served to us at the IIT dining hall had dozens of bugs on it. We ate after plucking the bugs off the surface of the cooked chapati.

Avinash is a naturally gifted teacher. John C. Hancock, then head of the electrical engineering department at Purdue University, who was visiting IIT, happened to attend his research seminar. He was so impressed that he offered Avinash a faculty appointment on the spot, even before the dissertation was written. Another of Indiresan's students, Arogyaswami Paulraj, from the Indian Navy, was to become a professor at Stanford University and invent MIMO systems that improved the performance of smart phones and other wireless devices.

I finished my Ph.D. in December 1970 and was immediately offered a teaching position. This happened so quickly that I did not give thought to other possibilities.

My research was initially on theoretical aspects of signal theory. The significant things I had done included the discrete version of the Hilbert transform and the sampling theorem for Walsh analysis. These results had applications to the emerging field of digital communications, where the challenge is to take a continuous waveform such as speech, sample it at regular intervals, and represent these samples in terms of binary bits while degrading the signal as little as possible.

I now got interested in mathematical symmetries in the application of information theory to quantum mechanics. My idea was that if quantum mechanics is associated with a fundamental uncertainty, a kind of a veiling, then perhaps this uncertainty is counterbalanced by new attributes.

In communications, information involves two parties—let's call them A, the sender, and B, the receiver. Both A and B know what the alphabet is, as in the case of transmission of text. Before the receipt of a letter in a sequence, there is an expectation related to the probability of each letter in the language used that may be calculated by counting their frequencies in a large text. Receipt of a letter with a lower probability communicates higher information, and this general idea has been used to design efficient systems for speech and images.

But the idea of information in physics is not a straightforward one. Is the information associated with an object to be attributed to a game between Nature and the human observer? Should it be measured by the number of stable states associated with the mathematical representation of the object? Does object information imply the existence of mind that goes beyond the awareness associated with the workings of the brain?

————

I was also interested in the philosophical problem of consciousness which had received much coverage in the media after the Kashmiri sage Gopi Krishna wrote an acclaimed autobiographical account of his spiritual journey. I got to meet him in Delhi and at his home in Srinagar during summer vacation. It was not too difficult to see that the phenomenon of consciousness cannot be explained scientifically but consideration of it brought focus on larger issues that are fundamental to the advancement of standard science.

I was to learn later of the subtle thinking of the Indian sages on this problem. They argued that consciousness is not a property of matter (for otherwise one will see it on display everywhere) and thus it must be a distinct ontological category.

Gopi Krishna was born in 1903 and I had heard of him first in 1967 during the Kashmir Pandit agitation. His autobiography, *Kundalini: The Evolutionary Energy in Man*, had received excellent reviews. His idea that spiritual advancement caused measurable neurophysiological changes was an intriguing hypothesis. It was embraced by Western scientists who were looking for scientific tests to check transformation in intelligence by meditation.

Gopi Krishna's grandson, Rakesh Kaul, was my student at IIT Delhi. Rakesh went on to become a successful businessman in the United States and he wrote a historical novel called The Last Queen of Kashmir.

As a member of the IIT faculty, I became quickly disillusioned. The weekly meeting in which topics were discussed to death until everybody said "yes" irked me the most. There was little scientific discussion, and no money for the faculty to present papers at national or international conferences.

In 1973, I was appointed the convener (director) of the first international systems conference that was to be held in IIT the following year, but its budget was pitifully small. At long last, the day arrived and I gave the welcome speech in the main hall of IIT. I also chaired a few sessions including one in which the Systems Society of India was born. We had participants from all over India and some from the US.

I made many good friends amongst colleagues. These included the husband-wife team of Rajendra and Krishna Arora, who worked on electromagnetics and signal processing, respectively. With Juzer Vasi, whose research was in semiconductor devices, I developed a course on history of science and technology that we called Science Dynamics. There were several other young staff members with fresh doctorates from American universities with whom I played Scrabble on weekend evenings.

Meanwhile, my sisters, Shakti and Jaishree, and younger brother, Neeraj, arrived at Jawaharlal Nehru University. This university, recently established during Indira Gandhi's administration, had become a center of leftist politics. Shakti was drawn to the Marxists and so, in my frequent visits to the campus, I got to know students who were to become prominent in the CPM (Communist Party Marxist), which dominated politics in West Bengal and Kerala for many years.

Communists in India have for most of their history served the interests of the Soviets or the Chinese. When Hitler attacked his erstwhile ally, the Soviet Union, in 1941, the fight against Germany became people's war for all communists. The Communist Party of India (CPI) was instructed by Moscow to take a position against the Quit India movement launched by Gandhi in 1942.

In 1948, within a few months of independence, the CPI claimed that India was ripe for armed revolution. The party expelled those who believed in accommodation with the progressive group within the Congress and organized the Telangana Rebellion that was put down in 1951.

The communists' suspicion of the Congress strengthened when Nehru dismissed the elected communist government in Kerala in the summer of 1959. Three years later, in 1962, during the China-India War, a section of the communists upheld the cause of China and portrayed India as the aggressor. It led eventually to a split in the CPI with the pro-Chinese faction leaving the parent party to form the Communist Party of India (Marxist) or CPM. The rump CPI remained loyal to the Communist Party of the Soviet Union.

At JNU, the university administration and the faculty were sympathetic to the CPM. Marxist students would speak of the impending dictatorship of the proletariat and the collapse of the West. This rhetoric was fine as a means to capture power, but the hollowness of the philosophy was evident. Why was the dictatorship of the elite of the Marxist party a good thing, when communist dictatorships elsewhere in the world had caused untold human suffering and death of millions?

The communists by privileging economics denied the spiritual and cultural dimensions to life. Communism conflated categories, speaking in the same breath of materialism and the psychological and subjective concept of exploitation. It had no answer to the practical problem of rational decision making by the bureaucrat, no matter how efficient, when faced with amounts of information beyond the capacity of the human brain. In the charged atmosphere of college politics at JNU, utopian ideas ruled supreme.

It was amusing that students, some of whom knew no Indian language and whose understanding of India was based on outdated colonial tracts, devoted their life to the capture of political power in India. But these children of privilege were not as impractical as one thought. There already existed a network for advancement in the Marxist-dominated world of academia.

The middle of the seventies was a story of endless political agitations that eventually ended with Prime Minister Indira Gandhi citing internal disturbance to declare Emergency Rule. This gave Mrs. Gandhi the authority to rule by decree wherein civil liberties were curbed, press was censored and most political opponents were imprisoned. The Emergency was in place for 21 months till its withdrawal on March 21, 1977 but for a large part of this period I was away in England and the United States.

I was at Imperial College in London during 1975-1976. My host in London was the electrical engineering professor Colin Cherry, who had written a fine book called *On Human Communication*, but we did not get to interact much as my interests had moved beyond classical communications theory in which he specialized.

My housing was arranged in Linstead Hall, located within Prince's Gardens, just across the road from the main South Kensington campus. I was required to eat there during weekdays and on weekend I would pick up dinner from one of the numerous Indian takeaways.

I spent my time either in the library soaking up books, walking around in the many parks nearby, visiting museums, and bookstores. I barely interacted with the Imperial College faculty although I was punctual in my daily checking of the mail at the office. The other visitor to the department at that time was Peter Elias from MIT and we bumped into each other in the hallway from time to time.

I made a few out-of-town trips that included Edinburgh, Cardiff, Stratford-upon-Avon, Leicester, and one trip via boat and coach to Paris and other cities along the way.

I was keen to explore symmetry to characterize information in an elementary particle, but this did not prove fruitful. I think my error was overdependence on mathematical formalism— this is what the physicist David Bohm, who was a professor at Birbeck College, told me.

I came to know Abdus Salam, originally from Pakistan, during this visit. He was much in the news, as the popular scientific media in Britain built up his case for the Nobel Prize. He commuted between London and Trieste in Italy where he was the director of an institute for theoretical physics.

Those were exciting days for physicists looking for a unified theory. The talk of a Theory of Everything was in the air, and Salam was a high priest of this field. Born in 1926 in Jhang in the Punjab, he got his Ph.D. from Cambridge when he was twenty-six, becoming full professor at Imperial College in 1957.

Salam's work was based on an imaginative synthesis of mathematical structures and in this style he followed his mentor Paul Dirac. He was also interested in mysticism and he took his religion of Ahmadi Islam very seriously.

He was intrigued by ancient Indian ideas. In one conversation with me, he brought up the question of the age of the universe given in the Purāṇas. He wanted to understand, if at all that was possible, how the present cycle in Purāṇic cosmology is about the same number as the estimate of the time of the Big Bang.

It is remarkable that he sought to bring opposites together in his mind, but this was at a high cost. He lived in two worlds and he wished to be faithful to both. He had simultaneous loyalties to Pakistan and his physics; to the traditions of his Rajput ancestry and his religion; and to his two wives, one Punjabi and the other English.

The proof of his dual loyalties is clear from his insistence that both his wives attend his Nobel award ceremony. This caused a diplomatic crisis for the hosts; the wives were ultimately seated in different places.

In his philosophy he tried to be loyal to physics where laws don't change with time and to the faith his Rajput forbears had adopted several centuries ago, where the prophet represents a unique break in time.

He may have felt his Ahmadi Muslim sect, which believes that prophets are sent by God time after time and Ghulam Ahmad (1839-1908) was such a person, was less in conflict with the ethos of physics than the orthodox interpretation of Islam, in which Muhammad's prophethood being the last is a pillar of the faith.

The Ahmadis (or the Ahmadiyya) believe that their founder, Mirza Ghulam Ahmad was prophet, promised messiah and Mahdi of Islam. As Salam's star in the world of physics rose, his sect came under increasing attack by the orthodoxy in Pakistan. The Ahmadis were declared non-Muslim by the Pakistani government in 1974.

Shortly after the partition, the Ahmadiyya community moved its headquarters from Qadian in India to Pakistan.

Upon expulsion from Islam in Pakistan, the Ahmadi leaders were exiled to London. As a minority religion in Pakistan, the Ahmadis remain a reviled group. Their educational institutions have been nationalized, and they are barred from holding public meetings.

The Ahmadiyya problem in Islam is characteristic of the schism in a religion that defines itself narrowly. The Ahmadiyyas say that they are true Muslims, whereas the orthodox clerics claim that by abandoning one of the principal beliefs of Islam, the Ahmadis have established a new religion and they should not have the right to call themselves Muslim.

Salam, as an observant religious Ahmadi Muslim, was aware of the ambiguity of his community's position. He responded to his expulsion by spending even more time in his pieties. But his enemies were relentless, and when he went to Pakistan after he had been awarded the Nobel Prize, he was barred from entering the premises of any university.

For Salam his sorrows did not end with his excommunication or death. In Pakistan he is a non-person and his name is not mentioned in textbooks. The popular press has concocted wild conspiracies of nuclear espionage against him.

His efforts in his waning years for the cause of science in Islamic countries came to naught. He had obtained pledges for a one-billion dollar fund, but when he and his coreligionists were banned from setting foot in Saudi Arabia, the sponsors withdrew.

———

I went to America in 1976 when I spent a summer working at Bell Laboratories in Murray Hill. The trip did not have auspicious beginning as an engine on our British Airways flight caught fire soon after we took off. The plane was able to turn around to Heathrow and as we landed we were met with screaming fire engines, the emergency doors opened and we slid down the escape chutes.

It was many hours before we were put on a new flight and since I had not had an opportunity to inform my cousin, Maharaj Kaul, in New York who was to pick me up at the airport. I was concerned about how I would reach his place. Thankfully, Maharaj and his wife Mohini were at the airport. They had heard about the fire on TV and found out the schedule of the relief flights bringing the stranded passengers.

I rented a room in Summit in New Jersey, the town near Bell Labs, where I would catch a bus to go to work and spent the weekends at Queens with Maharaj and Mohini.

Bell Labs at Murray Hill was then the world's premier place for research in communications and information. I was in the group that worked on creating new digital technologies for speech and images. My task was to develop a technique for scrambling of speech for telephones. I did this work with N.S. Jayant, a brilliant engineer from Bangalore (now Bengaluru) who was on the permanent staff of Bell Labs, and this work was eventually granted a patent.

Jayant was interested in theater and for some time he worked on a flexible schedule so that he could act in plays in New York City. Under the name Jayant Blue, he had a role in Mike Nichols's Comedians that played for over four months on Broadway.

The head of the acoustics research department was James Flanagan who was to receive the National Medal of Science in 1996. The work of Bell Lab facilitated the digital revolution. Its contributions included techniques of efficient digital representation of speech and pictures to send them quickly over wire or wireless that have made many of the key applications of the Web possible.

I visited Niagara Falls with Avinash who drove me next to Indiana where I saw the campus of his university. Lalita, my cousin in Washington, DC, took me to see Triloki Nath Kaul, the Indian ambassador, who was a wonderful host and we spent several hours at his home. Kaul had served earlier stints as ambassador to Moscow and as foreign secretary. He was a confidante of Indira Gandhi and one of the architects of the pro-Moscow policy of India.

He helped write the Panchsheel Agreement between India and China in the 1950s. In 1972, he assisted Indira Gandhi in formulating the Shimla Agreement with Pakistan in which both countries agreed to resolve their disputes through dialogue.

Upon his retirement as diplomat, he founded a journal called World Affairs and he invited me to write for it on more than one occasion. Jagdish Kapur, a Delhi entrepreneur, whom I got to know well later, eventually bought this journal and my writings for it continued for several years.

It was not just the tall buildings and huge bridges that impressed me on this visit to America; it was also the endless space and emptiness. Not knowing better, I took its spirit to be the counterpoint to my Kashmiri childhood, unfolded through ancient custom in small houses and narrow alleys of old places, hallowed by the memory of countless generations.

A few months after I returned to India, Indira Gandhi withdrew the Emergency. She announced mid-term elections but she had misjudged the mood of the voters. After a period of intense electioneering, Mrs Gandhi was soundly defeated and Morarji Desai became the new prime minister.

Back in India, the stark difference between the scientific culture at Bell Laboratories and IIT Delhi hit me.

Although the IITs had outstanding students, one couldn't say the same of most of its faculty. Many colleagures spent the day in idle conversation at long tea and lunch breaks. I felt isolated for I didn't have anyone to discuss science.

For some time, I turned my attention entirely to literature and wrote a couple of books of poetry that were published by the poet Purushottama Lal under his Writers Workshop imprint. I took my literary interests seriously and was to later write many other books of poetry both in English and Hindi but I shall not discuss it here for that story does not belong to the present book.

I was informed of the award of the Science Medal of the Indian National Science Academy in the autumn of 1977. Meanwhile, TIFR in Mumbai had offered me a one-month visiting appointment. At the end of it, I took the overnight train to Ahmedabad where at the Indian Science Congress I was to receive the medal personally from Prime Minister Morarji Desai.

Our accommodation had been taken care of by the Congress. I had just a few rupees left in Mumbai but didn't withdraw money from the bank thinking the substantial cash prize that I was to receive would be sufficient. As it happened, the prize was given as a check and there was no place at the Congress to cash it. Luckily, I ran into a girl volunteer who, when she learnt that I was a Kashmiri like her, invited me to her parents' home for dinner. The next day I took the train back to Delhi but as I had no money. I starved the entire day and reached home in the evening completely exhausted.

11. Marriage and America

I met Naumi in 1977. A lecturer of psychology in Kamla Nehru College, she was a Garhwali from Dehra Dun. A year later we decided to get married and the marriage took place in January 1979 in Delhi.

After schooling at Tara Hall in Shimla, Naumi (full name, Navnidhi Saklani) was the president of the student body at Indraprastha College and she finished clinical work in psychology in Bangalore. While teaching, she was also pursuing Ph.D. under the supervision of the noted psychoanalyst Sudhir Kakar. I had read Kakar's *The Inner World,* an exploration of Indian childhood and society that had received favorable reviews. But personally I thought his application of Freudian ideas, which had already been shown to be invalid by new research, to analyze the mind of the Indian child was pointless.

Naumi was born in Varanasi and her father, who had served for many years in the Indian Administrative Service, lived in Jakarta as director of the International Pepper Community. This had given her an opportunity to travel outside India. Her sister Pooja, who lived in Delhi, was married to a prominent young architect named Roopak Kothari.

We went to Udaipur for our honeymoon and then in summer took a vacation in Kashmir. Naumi was keen that we live in America for a few years and upon inquiry I received several offers. Of these, I chose a visiting professorship at

Louisiana State University in Baton Rouge that was changed to a regular professorial position the following year.

This, in Jimmy Carter's presidency, was a difficult time due to unemployment and rampant inflation, and I remember that one could get 18 percent annual interest on bank deposits. The signs of economic decline were all around for the logic of the economic and social policies set in motion after the Second World War had run its course. Carter's approach to the world was naïve and he was sanctimonious and humorless.

The path out of this was shown by UK's new Prime Minister Margaret Thatcher who assumed office in May 1979. She got parliament to make drastic changes to trade union laws introducing the regulation that unions must hold a ballot among members before calling strike.

Thatcher's economic policies promoted deregulation of the banks, flexible labor markets, and privatization of state-owned companies that cut down the power and influence of trade unions. But good policy is a sweet spot in between contending ideologies and she was to go too far with deregulation that cost her prime ministership.

Noticing the weakness of Carter, challenge to the United States arose all over the world. In Iran, the Shah, a staunch ally of the US, was overthrown and American diplomats were taken hostage by revolutionary guards in Tehran in November 1979. This hostage drama was the backdrop to the presidential campaign of 1980, and Carter's inept handling of the crisis paved the way for Ronald Reagan's victory. Knowing that Reagan would come down hard on them, the revolutionary guards let go of the hostages after 444 days, just before the new president took oath of office.

My undergraduate class in 1979 had a large cohort of Iranian students but after this no new students arrived from

Iran. The first couple of years of Reagan presidency were a continuation of economic difficulty but thereafter things changed and Reagan became a popular president, winning his re-election handily.

This was the time of explosive growth of computer technology and its applications to military, engineering and business processes. This industry required large number of programmers and engineers that the US was able to get from amongst the international students studying in its universities. There was no similar process by which the Soviet Union could get trained manpower which must have convinced its leaders that their challenge to America was doomed.

Indeed, a few years earlier one of the senior diplomats in the Soviet Embassy in Delhi invited me to dinner at his home. The invitation was sent to me through a colleague at IIT and we went to the dinner together. The diplomat broached the question of the economic race and how America was benefiting from the brain drain from India. I said that until the Soviets were to create an open society it held no attractions to the immigrant. I also mentioned the problems of the Soviet rule described in the writings of Boris Pasternak and Alexander Solzhenitsyn, many of whose books I had read.

Reagan used the advantage of computer technology to challenge the Soviet Union on all fronts including military hardware. He armed the Mujahedeen fighting the Soviets in Afghanistan and gave them Stinger missiles to shoot down planes. At some point the leadership in the Communist Party concluded that due to systemic reasons related to technology, America was pulling away ahead. But the stoking of religious hatreds by the United States was to have unintended consequences.

Soviet Union dissolved into its constituent units in 1991 during the presidency of George H.W. Bush. America was now the sole superpower. The strategic thinkers in the US now spoke of a unilateral globalized world, and the dawning of Pax Americana.

It was clear that the margins in manufacturing would shrink due to competition from low-wage countries. The political and business elite decided that the US will maintain its dominance of the world through military, finance, pharmaceuticals, information technology and entertainment.

I was impressed with many aspects of the organization of the American university. I liked my autonomy and checks and balances appeared to work even at the academic department.

The marketplace has a bearing on American university salaries, with departments such as business and medicine offering salaries higher than history of art or languages. But it is not entirely market-driven for tenure, obtained in six or seven years, makes the position permanent and it is difficult to dismiss tenured professors even if they are not productive. The American university is different from its counterparts in Europe, India or Australia, where salaries are determined by rank and seniority and do not vary across discipline.

Although, American universities remain the best in the world, they suffer from their own malaise. In the sciences, professors spend most of the time chasing grants and running from one fashionable area to another. In the arts, the faculty is divided into bitter ideological camps. The excellence of the American universities in the modern era is to be attributed to general prosperity and it is not clear how it will perform in adverse economic conditions.

———

Naumi worked as a clinical psychologist at a non-profit center in Baton Rouge for many years and she came to have a large circle of American friends.

Meanwhile, two children were born to us: Abhinav Gautam in 1982 and Arushi in 1986. It took us nearly four years to get our visa straightened and our first return to India was in 1983.

We sent our children to inner-city schools so that they would see the diversity of the American social world firsthand. As a boy, Abhinav was much interested in soccer and Arushi seemed to have talent for music and she learnt Hindustani classical vocal and Bharatanātyam for some time.

Abhinav was interested in music at college while he pursued a degree in biochemistry. He had his own gig as deejay in several clubs and he also wrote a column on techno music for a national magazine. On occasion he traveled out of town, deejaying in clubs in San Francisco and once in London. We were apprehensive as to where this will take him until we heard he had been accepted into medical college.

Arushi did her first degree in anthropology and then turned down admission in public health from several Ivy League universities to get into the lone medical school to which she had applied.

Both specialized in anesthesiology with residency in University of Miami and Tufts University, respectively.

———

After joining LSU, I took up random sequences, important in communications and cryptography, in continuation of my work at Bell Laboratories. Whereas my earlier work was specifically for speech security, I now analyzed random sequences from the perspective of number theory, examining the expansions of reciprocals of prime numbers. This is much more general than one thinks, for any periodic sequence can be derived from the ratio p/q where p and q are prime numbers.

The sequence 1/7 may be represented by its decimal expansion 142857 which repeats. In the binary case, one can generate the bits of the reciprocal 1/p by a formula. The sequence for 1/13 in the binary case is simply 00010011101. The period for such sequences is p-1 or a divisor, which is easy to see since in the long division by p, there can only be p-1 unique remainders. These sequences, or other similar random-looking sequences, can be used for addressing data to a specific customer and providing security in wireless communications.

At this time I was also working on several other problems of information transmission and cryptography and guest edited the very first special issue of IEEE Computer on data security in computer networks in 1983 and investigated various aspects of the newly emerged public key cryptography paradigm.

———————

Jaishree finished her Ph.D. at SUNY and got married in Stony Brook in 1982. We drove up from Baton Rouge to be at her wedding. After this she and her husband moved to Honolulu for jobs at the University of Hawaii. Neeraj and his wife, Lily, whom he had met in Delhi at JNU, were also doing their Ph.D. at Stony Brook but were then in India for fieldwork.

My parents came on their first visit to the United States in 1985. They arrived first in Baltimore where Neeraj was a post-doc at Johns Hopkins University. They were with us in Baton Rouge for several months and we took many picnic and vacation trips.

It was astonished that father and I had almost the same intuitions about the world. Jaishree had not been back to India for several years and she came down to Baton Rouge to visit us.

On this visit I urged father to write notes on his life and during the months he was with us, he wrote many pages in longhand. I typed them and they became the first draft of his autobiography.

It was in the mid-eighties that I started serious research on earliest Indian science. It began with my examination of Pāṇini's abstract grammar (5th century BCE) for Sanskrit that many consider equivalent in its form and shape to a computer program. I found it troubling that standard histories of India claimed that there was no writing at that time. It seemed incongruous that an illiterate culture will have the intellectual resources to create a subtle and powerful system that has continued to astonish scholars for over two millennia.

My study of Indian mathematical algorithms started with the kuṭṭaka method for solving algebraic equations that is in Āryabhaṭa's book of astronomy (about 500 CE). The power of this method was a revelation, and so I went back in time to the methods of building altars, which involve the solution of a variety of mathematical problems. It was clear that we were looking at a mathematically sophisticated civilization. The period of the altar construction was conservatively dated by scholars to about 1000 BCE, and historians accepted that the so-called Pythagoras theorem, which many consider the beginning of mathematics, was already known in India several centuries before its rediscovery in Greece.

Investigating Pāṇini and the modern subject of language understanding by computer, I argued that a Paninian approach to language analysis by computer could still be useful for certain applications.

The Sanskrit sphoṭa theory speaks of three parts of speech: paśyantī, madhyamā, and vaikharī, which are the vision, its enlargement in linguistic components, and the complete utterance, respectively. One may also speak of the reverse of this in the comprehension of speech. In reality, the sphoṭa idea applies to all human activity, including societal relationships and other creative expression and therefore is the foundation of semiotics. The linguist and semiotician Ferdinand du Saussure saw the applicability of these ideas to a whole range of human sciences including linguistics, philosophy, psychology, sociology and anthropology.

But there remains a gap between the vision and the final utterance, because the speaker must use phrases that belong to other contexts, and this is especially so of new experience. This is where poetry comes in because the poet uses different devices to create a sense that takes one beyond the words.

Another early Indian philosophical idea is that of Śabda Brahman where the source is seen as primal sound or energy that permeates the universe. This has lead to insights not only in the workings of sound within the mind but also in the very creation of the cosmos out of sound.

I was amazed at the sophistication of these ideas. The central intuition is that reality is transcendental, beyond full description by words, it and can only be apprehended intuitively. But one can, by the use of language, sharpen one's insight making it possible to take an intuitive leap beyond which one's insight is personal and inexpressible.

———

My examination of Vedic epistemology and philosophy of science culminated in the book *The Nature of Physical Reality* in 1986. The book's thesis was that paralleling the paradoxes of modern science, seen both in physics and logic, is the idea of parokṣa of the Upaniṣads. According to the Upaniṣads, reality cannot be fully described because all descriptions leave out the experiencing self and, therefore, knowledge is of two kinds: aparā (lower, linguistic, outer-object based) and parā (higher, related to the Self).

The book stressed that the paradoxes of modern science emerge out of the ill-defined relationship between the object and the observer. In the Upaniṣads the perceiving self is identified directly, whereas in modern science one speaks of the problem in a circuitous manner as in the paradoxes of logic.

The philosopher Debi Prasad Chattopadhyaya now wrote to me asking for a revised account of the epistemology of science and this became *The Architecture of Knowledge*. This book is an examination of the limits of science in dealing with the puzzle of consciousness.

One of the outstanding problems of ancient Indian history is the undeciphered Indus script. Scholars have worked on it for nearly a century, without success. As computer scientist and student of ancient history, I was drawn to it. A successful decipherment of Indus has the potential to revolutionize the understanding of ancient India.

The reading of long-forgotten scripts of the ancient world is a triumph of modern scholarship, which has led to the discovery of long-lost languages, bringing to light forgotten history, science and literature. Amongst the most celebrated successes is the decipherment of the Egyptian hieroglyphs that was helped by the discovery in 1799 of the

Rosetta Stone, an inscription in three languages. Several scholars contributed to the effort but the breakthrough was made by the Frenchman Jean-François Champollion.

More recently, the Mayan hieroglyphs were deciphered by the Russian Yuri Knorozov, revealing information about long-forgotten dynasties of Mesoamerica. Mayan writing was in use in Mesoamerica until the conquest by Spain. This literature was written in codices made of bark and other perishable media, and only four codices survived the campaign of destruction by Spanish missionaries. Other preserved texts in Mesoamerica are monumental inscriptions documenting rulership, conquest and calendrical and astronomical events.

In the Egyptian case, the same hieroglyphic sign can, according to context, be interpreted in diverse ways: a phonogram (phonetic reading), a logogram, or as an ideogram (determinative that defines semantic reading). The determinative differentiates the word from its homophones. Most non-determinative signs are phonetic in nature, which means that the sign is read independent of its visual allusion.

Egyptian writing is a syllabic writing system, supplemented by logographs. In most written words, a glyph block represents a word and within it symbols are used for syllables. There are occasional symbols that represent complete words. Symbols that represent one consonant are called uniliteral signs, those representing two consonants are biliteral signs, and those standing for three signs are triliteral.

Twenty-four uniliteral signs make up the basic hieroglyphic alphabet. Unlike cuneiform, which was used in Mesopotamia and Old Persia, Egyptian hieroglyphic writing does not normally indicate vowels.

Most work on the decipherment of the Indus script has been vitiated by preconceived ideas. There are two main theories related to the language: the first takes it to be Dravidian, and the second takes it to be Aryan. In the eighties the Dravidian language decipherers were finding things that they had already assumed in the texts. Naturally, these purported decipherments went nowhere.

Early writing systems such as Sumerian, Egyptian, and Chinese used pictographic signs to represent many objects based on the rebus principle, where the homophone of an abstract word is used for its representation. Using the rebus principle, one may use the picture of an eye to represent the personal pronoun "I", or the picture of waves (sea) to represent the word "see". In Sumerian script, the arrow was assigned the phonetic value "ti" for this word means "arrow".

The would-be Indus decipherers took the main picture signs of the Indus script and started looking for corresponding words in Tamil or its old supposed forms to set the corresponding phonetic value. The proposal was made that the name for fish in proto-Dravidian is *min* which is also the word for "star". Then six vertical strokes followed by fish sign should refer to the Pleiades and a whole mythology related to the constellation in the sky was imagined.

But there are also more frequent two vertical strokes and three vertical strokes before the fish sign and, therefore, the six-star identification is arbitrary and a dead-end. One could even use this method mischievously by arguing that a fish is able to cross a tank or the sea and, therefore, its rebus basis should be "tāra" that also stands for "star" in Sanskrit and this identification can be pushed in all sorts of directions.

Plausibility is not enough. A successful decipherment should rule out competing decipherments, which the proposals did not do.

Archaeologists agree that there is continuity of cultural artifacts between the Harappan and the later historical period even if there is a gap in the periods of Indus and Brahmi writing (and this gap is being shrunk by new finds). It is also agreed that the Harappan culture was multi-ethnic and possibly multi-lingual. Given all this, the worst a person can do is to assume a solution before even starting, as was done by those who were looking for a Dravidian solution.

The line I took in my investigation was to analyze the relationship between the signs of the Indus and the later Brahmi script, which is the parent of nearly all Indian, Southeast Asian, and East Asian scripts. This is sensible also because Brahmi is the script of both the earliest Sanskrit and Tamil inscriptions.

I considered the ten most frequently occurring Indus signs and compared them with the ten most common Brahmi signs and found that structurally they looked nearly identical at the same rank.

I also looked at the endings of the Indus texts and found that they corresponded to the genitive case of the corresponding Brahmi texts from the historical period. So on structural grounds one could assert that the Brahmi script was genetically connected to the Indus script.

Even the Indus signs for 5 and 10, identified based on their occurrence with small groups of vertical strokes, are similar to the signs in Brahmi. The fish sign represented 10 in Brahmi, before the development of the symbol for zero, and it appears to do so in Indus as well.

If my work is correct, the similarities between Brahmi and Semitic scripts can be explained through their derivation from the Indus script. The agents for this could be the Indo-Aryan Mitanni who ruled West Asia for centuries in the second millennium BCE reaching the zenith of their power in the fourteenth century. Details of the Mitannis are known to us through the celebrated excavations in Amarna in Egypt in early twentieth century.

I wrote several articles on this problem for an American journal called Cryptologia, in which I examined the structural relationships, as well as for the Indian Journal for the History of Science in which I provided an overview of the evolution on early Indian writing.

12. Discovery of Vedic Astronomy

The study of ancient mathematics led me to the astronomy of the Vedic period. There are different kinds of data with astronomical clues. For starters, we have the alignment of monumental buildings with cardinal directions that can reveal information about the era of construction for the precession of the earth shifts these directions. A link between altar geometry and astronomy has the potential to decode references of chronological significance.

The precession of the earth shifts the seasons at a rate of about a month every two thousand years. Some Vedic notices mark the beginning of the year by the vernal equinox in Orion which was astronomically true for around 4500 BCE. Other astronomical references point to later time periods, indicating a long period of time over which astronomy developed into a science.

Fire altars, with astronomical basis, have been found in the third millennium cities of India. The texts that describe their designs are conservatively dated to the first millennium BCE, but their contents appear much older. Basing his analysis on the Pythagorean triples in Greece, Babylon, and India, the historian of science A. Seidenberg concluded that the knowledge contained in the Indian Śulba Sūtras goes back to at least 1700 BCE even if the texts themselves are of a later date. The Vedāṅga Jyotiṣa (VJ), which describes some of the astronomical knowledge of the times of altar ritual, has an internal date of c. 1350 BCE, obtained from its assertion that the winter solstice was at the asterism Śraviṣṭhā (Delphini).

The design details of the altars are given in the Vedic texts, and some of the numbers in the designs code fractions of the year. I was also aware that the Ṛgveda itself had been described at one place as an altar of mantras.

But the solution to this puzzle and my discovery of the astronomy of the Ṛgveda came rather suddenly in a flash in early November 1992.

The Vedic corpus that includes the Vedic Saṃhitās, the Brāhmaṇas, the Āraṇyakas, the Upaniṣads, and the Sūtras covers a vast time span. The Epics are coeval with the last stage of the Vedic period and the Purāṇas also contain very old material.

Sanskritic people in West Asia during the second millennium BCE, most likely emigrants from India, could be the explanation for certain commonalities in Indian and Babylonian astronomy. Since the Sanskritic names of the elite in West Asia are Indo-Aryan and not Iranian, the most plausible basis is to take them to be descended from emigrants who moved west after the drying up of the Sarasvati River that is dated to around 1900 BCE.

The archaeological record shows continuity and the new field of DNA dating of ancient migrations shows that there is no break in the Indian genetic record, contradicting the earlier idea of large scale invasions from outside. In a well-regarded synthesis of the evidence, Stephen Oppenheimer argued that the peopling of Europe occurred by a northwest migration out of India and Iran around 40,000 years ago. The idea in the genetic synthesis is that modern humans came to India about 80,000 years ago and 40,000 years later one group left India for Central Asia and Europe and another for northeast Asia.

Indian astronomy speaks of ages of successive longer durations, which is an example of the pervasive idea of recursion, or repetition of patterns across space, scale and time. An example of this is the division of the ecliptic into 27 star segments (nakṣatras), with which the moon is conjoined in its monthly circuit, each of which is further sub-divided into 27 sub-segments (upa-nakṣatras), and the successive divisions of the day into smaller measures of 30 units.

The idea of recursion is embodied in Indian art, providing an archaeoastronomical window on sacred and monumental architecture. It appears that this was an old idea because intricate spiral patterns are also found in the paintings of the Mesolithic period.

Vedic ritual was based on the times for the full and the new moons, solstices and the equinoxes. There were two years: the ritual year started with the winter solstice (mahāvrata), and the civil one started with the spring equinox (viṣuva). The passage of the rising of the sun in its northward course from the winter solstice to the summer solstice (viṣuvant) was called gavām ayana, or the sun's walk. The solar year was divided into two ayanas: in the uttarāyaṇa, the sun travels north; in the dakṣiṇāyana, it travels south. The calendar used for festivals and religious observances still follows this system.

In addition to the movement of the moon marked by nightly conjunction with one of the 27 or 28 nakṣatras, the Ṛgveda 1.164 speaks of another tradition of dividing the circuit of the sun (zodiac) into twelve equal parts called the Ādityas. The incommensurability between the lunar and the solar reckonings led to the search for ever-increasing cycles to synchronize the motions of the sun and the moon, and this is how the yuga astronomical model was born. In the lunar month, there were separate traditions of counting the beginning of the month by the full-moon day and the new-moon day.

During the earliest times in India there existed a centennial calendar with a cycle of 2,700 years. Called the Saptarṣi calendar, it is still in use in Kashmir. Its current beginning is taken to be 3076 BCE. Greek historians Pliny and Arrian suggest that the calendar used in India began in 6676 BCE. It is most likely that this calendar was the Old Saptarṣi calendar with a beginning at 6676 BCE. Other major Indian eras that have wide currency are Kaliyuga (3102 BCE), Vikrama (58-57 BCE), and Śaka (78 CE).

The shifting of seasons through the year makes it possible to date several statements in the Vedic books. The Śatapatha Brāhmaṇa statement that the Kṛttikā never swerve from the east corresponds to 2950 BCE. The Maitrāyaṇīya Brāhmaṇa Upaniṣad refers to the winter solstice being at the mid-point of the Śraviṣṭhā (Delphini) segment and the summer solstice at the beginning of Māgha. This indicates 1660 BCE. The changes in the beginning of the Nakṣatra lists come down to the time of Varāhamihira (550 CE) when the vernal equinox was in Aśvini.

The foundation of Vedic cosmogony is the notion of *bandhu* (homologies or binding between the outer and the inner). In the Āyurveda medical system associated with the Vedas, the 360 days of the year were taken to be mapped to the 360 bones of the developing fetus, which later fuse into the 206 bones of the person.

I discovered that the Indians had estimated correctly that the sun and the moon are approximately 108 times their respective diameters from the earth (perhaps from the angular size of a pole removed 108 times its height being the same as the angular size of the sun and the moon), and this number was used in sacred architecture. The distances to the sanctum sanctorum of the temple from the gate and the perimeter of the temple were taken to be 54 and 180 units, which are one-half each of 108 and 360.

Owing to assumed recursion, 108 appears as the number of beads in the japamālā (telling of beads is to make a symbolic journey across the worlds), the number of dance movements of the Nāṭya Śāstra, the names of the God and the Goddess, the number of pilgrimages, the number of spiritual masters, and so on. There are also 108 divisions of the zodiac and 108 rhythmical patterns (tālas) of music. With the human body described by a measure of 108, the weak points of the body are counted in the Āyurveda system to be 107.

The sacred ground for Vedic ritual is the precursor to the temple. The altar ritual was associated with the east-west axis and its origins can be traced to priests who maintained different day counts with respect to the solstices and the equinoxes. Specific days were marked with ritual observances that were done at different times of the day.

In the ritual at home, the householder employed three altars that are circular (earth), half-moon (atmosphere), and square (sky), which are like the head, the heart, and the body of the Cosmic Man (puruṣa). In the Agnicayana, the great ritual of the Vedic times that forms a major portion of the narrative of the Yajurveda, the atmosphere and the sky altars are built afresh in a great ceremony to the east. This ritual is based upon the Vedic division of the cognitively experienced universe into three parts of earth, atmosphere, and sky with assigned numbers of 21, 78, and 261, respectively.

The numerical mapping is maintained by placement of 21 pebbles around the earth altar, sets of 13 pebbles around each of 6 intermediate (13×6=78) altars, and 261 pebbles around the great new sky altar called the Uttara-vedi, which is built in the shape of a falcon; these numbers add up to 360, which is symbolic representation of the year. The proportions related to these three numbers, and others related to the observed motions of the planets, and angles related to the sightings of specific stars are reflected in the plans of the temples of the historical period.

––––––––

There is a modern analog to the Vedic idea of interconnections. This is the idea of inner biological clocks. Living organisms have rhythms that are matched to the periods of the sun or the moon. There are quite precise biological clocks of 24-hour (according to the day), 24 hour 50 minutes (according to the lunar day since the moon rises roughly 50 minutes later every day) or its half representing the tides, 29.5 days (the period from one new moon to the next), and the year. Monthly rhythms, averaging 29.5 days, are reflected in the reproductive cycles of many marine plants and those of animals. The menstrual period is a synodic month and the average duration of pregnancy is nine synodic months. There are other biological periodicities of longer durations.

It is most fascinating that the astronomy of the fire altars was coded in the organization of the Ṛgveda, which was taken to be a symbolic altar of hymns. The code of the Ṛgveda is of unique significance since this ancient book has been preserved with incredible fidelity by remembering the text not only as a sequence of syllables (and words) but also through several different permutations of these syllables.

The number of syllables in the Ṛgveda confirms the textual references that the book was to represent a symbolic altar. According to various early texts, the number of syllables in the Ṛgveda is 432,000, which is the number of muhūrtas (1 day = 30 muhurtas) in forty years. In reality the syllable count is somewhat less because certain syllables are supposed to be left unspoken.

The verse count of the Ṛgveda can be viewed as the number of "sky days" in forty years or 261 × 40 = 10,440, and the verse count of all the Vedas is 261 × 78 = 20,358.

―――――

The dissemination of the discovery of Vedic astronomy to the wider community was facilitated by its mention in Klaus Klostermaier's well-known book *A Survey of Hinduism* in 1993. Klostermaier, a German-Canadian, had lived in India for several years in the 1960s that resulted in his appointment at the Vatican as advisor on non-Christian religions. An ordained Catholic priest, he was a professor of religious studies at the University of Manitoba in Canada.

When I wrote to him with my findings, he immediately wrote back saying, "I had suspected for a long time that there was something to the Ṛgveda which went far beyond what our philology and history could read out. Here it is! [This is an] epoch-making discovery." Thereafter, he made a point to mention this work in his many books on Hinduism.

David Frawley was an enthusiastic supporter calling it "a monumental accomplishment." Many other scholars both in the West and India felt that this was a major advance with the potential to explain many puzzles of Indian civilization.

In Delhi, I received encouragement from Kapila Vatsyayan, the director of the Indira Gandhi National Center for the Arts and the Buddhist scholar and linguist Lokesh Chandra. Kapilaji was a prominent scholar and administrator in the field of the arts. Lokeshji, the son of the linguist and politician Raghu Vira, was likewise a star in the firmament of Delhi's intellectual scene. I also received much encouragement from the sage and scholar Ram Swarup. Sita Ram Goel published the first edition of the book on the astronomical code.

Kapilaji invited me to speak at her institute, where I met the Tantra scholar Madhu Khanna and the poet Kailash Vajpeyi, and to a conference titled Rūpa Pratirūpa: Mind, Man and Mask in 1998 where I met the musicologist Prem Lata Sharma, who had been Vice-Chancellor of the Indira Kala Sangeet Vishwavidyalaya at Khairagarh. I was gratified when she postponed her return to Banaras, where she lived with her sister (who was accompanying her), so that she could hear me the next day. We corresponded after my return to the United States but she was to pass away later that year.

The Rūpa Pratirūpa conference brought together other scholars from a variety of fields. This is where I first met the anthropologist David Napier, the actor and director Maharaj Krishna Raina, the historian of art Munish Chandra Joshi, the scholar of drama Bharat Gupt, and the archaeologist Brij Mohan Pande.

––––––––––

Swami Rama, a prominent yoga master in the United States, had established the Himalayan Institute in Honesdale in Pennsylvania that published many finely produced books on Indian wisdom and conducted yoga and meditation courses. He was famous as the first yogi who showed doctors that the involuntary nervous system could be controlled. Researchers at the Menninger Foundation in Topeka, Kansas, in 1970 had seen him produce delta brain waves, associated with deep sleep, while keeping track of whatever was going on in the room; he could also control his heartbeat and develop a large temperature difference across two points in his palm.

This was revolutionary as far as standard medical science was concerned. No wonder, Encyclopedia Britannica and Nature Science Annual did major stories on him in their annual review of science for 1973. When asked about his feats, he said: "All of the body is in the mind, but not all of the mind is in the body."

Naumi told me that he was from Uttarakhand and her family knew him, so I wrote to him. He replied he was very interested in my Vedic discoveries and invited me for a visit. At his ashram, I learnt first-hand of the good work his Institute had done in spreading spiritual knowledge. He had impeccable taste, the imprint of which was in all things at the ashram.

Swami Rama was to found a medical university near Dehra Dun, not far from Rishkesh, in his later years and I visited him there before his death in 1996.

I was also invited to run annual short courses on my work at Arsha Vidya Gurukulam, a Vedic school at Saylorsburg, Pennsylvania, that was established by Swami Dayananda Saraswati. Swamiji was a brilliant speaker with a fine sense of humor. He started out as a disciple of Swami Chinmayananda, the founder of the Chinmaya Mission that has had much influence bringing Vedic knowledge to the world.

Around this time I began receiving correspondence from the mathematician Emilio Spedicato of University of Bergamo in Italy. He was an amateur historian who wished to understand the connections between ancient India and Europe. He invited me to his university and I used this opportunity to travel through Italy with Naumi and Arushi.

I had written occasional articles for newspapers for many years. Now I began to write regular columns for two online publictions. This led to valued friendships with other columnists, in particular Varsha Bhosle, the daughter of the singer Asha Bhosle, and Rajeev Srinivasan, a fine writer of uncompromising integrity.

13. In Search of the Observer

The year 1992 was particularly productive for me. I made three important discoveries. First, I discovered the long-forgotten astronomy of the Vedic period with implications for our understanding of Indian culture. In particular, I had found that the very organization of the Ṛgveda has a unique structure that codes information in a fashion similar to the fire altars. This showed that there was a scientific basis to the ritual, which served as sacred theater communicating different meanings to the participants based on their attainment.

Second, I discovered a method for training an instantaneously trained neural network where the objective was to map specific inputs and their generalization to different classes. In this I had been able to go beyond the backpropagation algorithm. My network could be used in the design of artificial intelligence machines, and I was to receive a US patent for this invention. If indeed the brain works like neural network models, then this network could explain short-term memory. The training of standard neural networks using backpropagation took a long time and, therefore, unlike my model they could not explain short-term memory.

Third, I found an interesting mechanism in a feedback neural network, so that an activity originating at a single neuron can lead to a unique pattern. This could then explain how neuroscientists have in experiments found that stimulation of a single neuron triggers a specific memory.

The area of feedback networks became popular when a Caltech chemist by name John Hopfield suggested that one could mathematically investigate the properties of a neural network (which are binary in behavior) in about the same way we study properties of assemblies of atoms that are also characterized by binary property, namely that of magnetization. He suggested that the final stable state of the solid is determined by the minimization of an energy function and so one could consider feedback neural network dynamics as a minimization problem.

I showed that if the state of just a single neuron were fixed, it could then force neighboring neurons into appropriate state which will in turn spread the activity in a manner that the state of the entire assembly is uniquely determined. The technical papers on these findings were published in scholarly journals the following year.

Soon afterward, I co-founded and co-chaired a series of International Conferences on Computational Intelligence and Neuroscience that were held mostly in North Carolina but also traveled elsewhere. We invited the world's leading neuroscientists to speak at the conference.

———

From a logical perspective, there is a divide between the inanimate world governed by physical law and conscious beings who are certain they have freedom. Also, Nature appears to behave strangely when observers interact with it.

The difficulty is most acute when considering the framework of quantum theory that tries to reconcile observations on light and atomic particles that exhibit wave and particle behavior under different circumstances. It is usual to view light as an electromagnetic wave, but at other times it makes sense to see it as a stream of particles called photons.

In Young's double-slit experiment, light emitted from a source in front of the slits creates interference patterns on the screen behind the slits. We cannot view it purely as the interference of different waves passing through the slits since it happens even if the laser source is of such weak intensity that it only emits one photon at a time. If interference is the basis, then each photon must be taken to pass through both the slits at the same time! If any one of the two slits is blocked, the interference pattern disappears.

The interference pattern persists if photons are replaced by electrons. Since electrons have mass, it is difficult to reconcile the idea of self-interference of an electron passing through both the slits with common sense. When attempt is made to determine whether the electron went through a specific path, the interference does not occur. It is as if the electron does not *wish* for the experimenter to know how it has traveled.

Quantum mechanics assumes that an isolated system evolves in a deterministic fashion if it is left alone. A quantum state is different from a classical state in that it can be a superposition of several mutually exclusive components and therefore the particle should be seen as going through both slits, which is not a mystery if its fundamental basis is wavelike. A classical shirt in solid color can only be, say, blue or red or yellow. A quantum shirt, on the other hand, can be blue, red, and yellow at the same time. This idea of superposition is a carry-over from wave phenomena. The other basic axiom of quantum theory is that upon measurement the state collapses to one of its component states.

———

The philosophical framework for quantum mechanics is provided by the so-called Copenhagen Interpretation. This is a positivist view of reality according to which one can only speak of results of experiments and not of a reality that is independent of observers. The state function of the quantum object expresses the experimenter's knowledge of the object and it does not have an independent reality. It is the nature of experimentation that not all properties of the system can be determined at the same time and the unknown properties must be described by probabilities.

The Copenhagen Interpretation takes wave-particle duality to be an inherent characteristic of matter. Some experimental arrangements show the particle-like properties of matter and some others the wave-like properties. In other words, the geometry of the experimental situation determines which of the two aspects will characterize the measurement.

Our senses and the results of physics experiments are defined in the classical world where mutually exclusive properties cannot be seen at the same time. The experimental apparatus, therefore, reduces the potential knowledge encapsulated in the wave function to a specific value.

At a deeper level, the Copenhagen Interpretation is based on the idea of psychophysical parallelism. This means that there are two parallel entities, the physical world and the mind, and one cannot be reduced to the other. But then what is mind? How do we relate it to brain processes? These are questions to which I was to devote much attention.

The Copenhagen Interpretation is most widely accepted in the physics community. But its acknowledgment of limits on what can be known and privileging of the observer has irked many scientists and other interpretations have been proposed of which the Many Worlds Interpretation has had some influence in recent years.

———

The supporters of the Many Worlds Interpretation (MWI) believe that the universe itself has its own wave function that evolves in a deterministic way. This avoids the problem of the collapse of the wave function for after the measurement the apparatus gets into an entanglement with the system. What we finally observe is a consequence of decoherence from this entangled state.

The idea of MWI comes from an application of the ensemble view of probability to the measurement process. An ensemble is a collection of possibilities associated with a process and it is more than any specific realization of it. Therefore, the measurement leads to outcomes that can only be determined probabilistically. In some versions of MWI it is assumed that the world splits into many copies so that taken as an ensemble the behavior is determined completely by the probability distribution associated with the measurement variable.

If the Copenhagen Interpretation is an inside-out view of the universe where the reality is constructed out of the perceptions of the experimenter, MWI is an outside-in view in which the mathematical function of the universe, and its sub-functions, represent the primary reality.

———

One prominent quantum theoriest I had the pleasure of meeting many times since the mid-seventies is George Sudarshan. Born in 1931 in Kerala, he graduated from the Madras Christian College, receiving his Ph.D. degree from the University of Rochester in 1958.

Sudarshan has made significant contributions to several areas of physics. He was the originator (with Robert Marshak) of the V-A theory of the weak force (also done later by Richard Feynman and Murray Gell-Mann), which eventually paved the way for the electroweak theory. He also developed a quantum representation of coherent light.

Sudarshan's significant contribution to the field of quantum optics is a theorem proving the equivalence of classical wave optics to quantum optics. He proposed the so-called Sudarshan-Glauber representation that predicts optical effects that are purely quantum, which cannot be explained classically.

Sudarshan was the first to propose the existence of tachyons, particles that travel faster than light. He developed formalism called dynamical maps that is useful to study the theory of open quantum system. He also proposed the quantum Zeno effect that shows how the experimenter, by the mere act of repeated observation, can freeze the evolution of a physical system. Could this be the model for how consciousness influences physical world?

There is general support for the view that he missed out on receiving Nobel Prize two times. First for the work on weak theory because that paved way for the electroweak theory for which Steven Weinberg, Sheldon Glashow, and Abdus Salam received the prize. Second for the work on quantum optics related to the Sudarshan-Glauber representation, for which Roy J. Glauber won a share of the prize.

Sudarshan and I met many times at Vedanta Congresses, run by Rama Rao Pappu at Miami University in Oxford, Ohio. This Congress, which was run annually (sometimes even more frequently), was a place where philosophers of Vedanta and scientists met to exchange their insights.

In one of these meetings, Sudarshan told me that Ram Chandra Kak, the prime minister of Jammu and Kashmir during 1945-1947, had profound influence on his worldview. Apparently, R.C. Kak invited Sudarshan to a vacation in Dachigam in Kashmir when Sudarshan was in the limelight in the sixties for his hypothesis of tachyons.

Ram Chandra Kak told Sudarshan of his belief in a web of life. Specifically, he said how when he was the chief archaeologist of Jammu and Kashmir, an astrologer told him that he was destined to be the Prime Minister. It was an unlikely possibility that had come true.

I published a paper in 2007 on a fundamental paradox of information. The paradox is: if the universe at the time of "big bang" was regular and it had correspondingly small information, what is the source of the complexity of the universe at present time? Viewed as a quantum system, the entropy of the universe should not change.

I argued that the measure of quantum entropy due to John von Neumann, which is currently used for this problem, is not appropriate for examining the amount of information that can be provided by Nature to the observer. I proposed a new measure that depends on the relationship between the system and its observer, showing how the evolution of the universe can be seen to transform one kind of entropy to another.

This was more than an abstruse mathematical exercise, for it brought into focus the role of sentient agents. In my view, entropy has two components: one informational (related to the pure components of the quantum state), and the other that is thermodynamic (which is receiver independent). The receiver can estimate the unknown state

132

by adjusting the basis vectors so that he gets closer to the unknown state. The information that can be obtained from such a state in repeated experiments is potentially infinite in the most general case.

This approach is consistent with the view that one cannot speak of information associated with a system excepting in relation to an experimental arrangement together with the protocol for measurement. The experimental arrangement is integral to the amount of information that can be obtained.

14. TROUBLED TIMES

In the late 80s, I wrote general articles on current events for India Abroad, a New York based weekly, which must have been widely read, because in 1988 I heard from the Indian Consul in New York that India's then Prime Minister Rajiv Gandhi, who was coming on an official visit to the United States, wished to have breakfast with me.

I thought about it and decided not to attend because it was a lot of trouble and expense flying to New York City from Louisiana and I was not sure if I had anything valuable to say. But this became a motivation for me to understand the changes taking place in India.

These were troubled time for India. A Sikh revolt was brewing in the Punjab and there were frequent incidents of murder and massacre of bus passengers. The revolt was managed and financed by Pakistan's secretive intelligence agency ISI, which became emboldened by its use by America to fight its proxy war in Afghanistan against the Soviets.

The beginning of the revolt had its birth in the opposition amongst some Sikhs to the popularity the Nirankari sect achieved in the seventies. This sect of Sikhism did not insist on outer symbols. My aunt, Aruna Kaul, became a follower and my mother also attended many meetings. The Nirankaris spoke of formless divinity and their meetings, unlike traditional religious meetings with sermons, were participatory with singing of bhajans and dancing.

The Sikh religious establishment, feeling threatened, began a campaign against the Nirankaris accusing their leader of being an agent of the government to neutralize Sikh political power. There were armed clashes between the two groups and eventually on April 24, 1980, the leader of Nirankaris, Baba Gurbachan Singh, was assassinated. The police charged associates of a young Sikh priest Jarnail Singh Bhindranwale with the crime.

After the murder of their master, the Nirankaris faded. Violence had silenced them. Bhindranwale, established in Golden Temple in Amritsar, broadcast calls for independence of Punjab. Meanwhile, bands of militants began attacking policemen, government and army officials, and there were random murders of Hindus.

In 1984, Prime Minister Indira Gandhi sent in the Army to clear the temple of the militants. Bhindranwale and his associates were killed, but in the battle the temple complex was damaged and there were many deaths, which outraged the Sikhs. Two months later, in October 1984, Indira Gandhi's Sikh bodyguards assassinated her. Rajiv Gandhi, Indira Gandhi's son, succeeded her as prime minister.

Mobs took to the streets of Delhi following Indira Gandhi's murder and several thousand Sikhs were killed. The militancy continued for years before peace was restored in the mid-1990s.

In 1986, I was in India as a UNDP expert and spent a couple of weeks of that period in Srinagar. Father and mother came along and it was great to go see places connected with my childhood. But we could see signs of simmering disquiet.

While the Punjab was on the boil, extremist groups in Kashmir organized ethnic cleansing of Kashmiri Hindus starting in 1989. The Soviet Union had collapsed, primarily due to the decade long insurgency in Afghanistan in which the Stinger missiles supplied to the mujahedeen downed many Soviet planes and helicopters.

Pakistani strategic thinkers thought that a similar strategy would make India get out of Kashmir. Within a year hundreds of selective and random murders forced nearly all Hindus, who comprised less than five percent of the population of the Vale, to flee their homes.

In areas of Jammu where the population was mixed assassins from Pakistan murdered many hoping others would leave. There were killings elsewhere in India, including the burning of pilgrims in the Godhra train and attacks on Akshardham and Varanasi. To force the few Kashmiri Hindus who had stayed on in their villages, 23 people from different families were shot in Wandhama on 25th January 1998. In Nadimarg on 23rdMarch 2003, 24 people were killed.

It was chilling to read news of one atrocity or another somewhere in India. In some ways it was similar to terrorism in Europe in recent years.

This campaign of terror was nowhere as widespread and sustained as in Kashmir. The Hindus fled their homes and took refuge wherever they could, with their lives shattered forever. As refugees, hundreds of miles away from their homes, they were housed in one-room hovels in Jammu. I was invited to give a speech at a meeting called by young Kashmiris in Jammu in December 1991 to reflect on what should be done. I got an opportunity to see first-hand the condition of the refugees, and it was heartbreaking.

The youth established an organization called Panun Kashmir and they declared as their goal the unrealistic idea of a homeland for the Hindus within the valley. This was more a cry of helplessness than anything else.

15. Losing Father

Father and mother came again to the United States in 1992. They were first in Rockville, Maryland, with Neeraj and Lily, and I was able to be there on my father's 75th birthday in October. It seemed idyllic to see my parents doing well and happy with their grandchildren, relatives and friends.

They were in Baton Rouge for a few months in early 1993. This is when father resumed work on his autobiographical notes after a hiatus of nearly seven years. We had great conversations for hours every evening on all kinds of subjects. For our children it was something I myself had never experienced since I grew up long after my grandparents had died.

Finally they went to Honolulu to see Jaishree. They had been there for just over a month, when the thunderbolt struck. I received the call from Jaishree in my office as I was preparing to teach a class. Leaving our children with a friend, Naumi and I managed to get to Honolulu by nightfall. Mother was crying inconsolably. She and father had gone down to the swimming pool and suddenly he felt unwell. He went up to the apartment and rested. When he awoke, he had light dinner and went to bed and then at night he had a heart attack. The ambulance took him to the hospital but it was too late.

The next day Avinash arrived and then Neeraj and Lily. It was very painful to get used to the idea that father was no more.

Father was the sweetest person one could imagine. He was mellow and I never saw him lose his temper. He was thoughtful and kind to everyone and he expected us to be likewise. As an avid reader he was well informed about current affairs and ancient history.

Mother was not prepared for it because father had never been ill all his life and she was only 64. Maybe he had some kind of a premonition. In Baton Rouge a couple of months earlier, I asked him if he was ready for the knee replacement surgery. He said not before his next birthday in October, adding that if he made it to it he was going to live for another 14 years.

After the funeral we rented a boat and scattered the ashes in the sea. Mother kept herself busy in Jaishree's apartment cooking for not only her children but sundry other guests who dropped in.

rātas osum lav zan lärith
subahas pravi ketha trävith gom

At night he was with me like dew drop on flower
At morning's first ray he fled leaving me alone.
-- Arnimal

A month later, she traveled with Jaishree and Vajra together with father's ashes back to Delhi. Next month we went to Haridwar to immerse the ashes in the Ganga River.

The following year, in 1994, mother agreed to go back to Hawaii for six months. She wished to know if living in Hawaii with Jaishree was a realistic option. The obvious negatives were that she did not know English well and Jaishree did not have a large social circle.

Each weekday afternoon she would walk over to the park near the local pharmacy and sit on a bench and watch people. While on the bench she called me every day. She loved going out to the shopping malls and to the beach.

During the winter holidays, Naumi and I and the children went to Hawaii for a few days. Shakti had also arrived to spend the vacations. We went to Maui and drove to the peak of the Haleakala volcano.

katha gai nenglith atha rūzith
kan china tas ben hekan būzith
sankalpan hund kor sanīyas

Struck dumb and with frozen hands
We can hear nothing but him
Our resolves are forgotten.
—Krishna Joo Razdan

Over the next few years, Jaishree took upon herself to translate Lalla's verses, writing a couple of books on them. Mother had always loved Lalla and sang her verses when we were children. She was delighted that she could help Jaishree with the meaning of obscure words.

16. PHILOSOPHY AND TANTRA

My book on the astronomy of the Ṛgveda appeared in Delhi in 1994. Meanwhile, my friend from New Mexico, David Frawley, suggested that we write a book together for the general public and we recruited the well-known yoga author Georg Feuerstein to be a co-author. This book was put together in a few months and published by Quest Books in 1996. It won several awards for its production and in some time German, Italian, and Korean translations appeared. The Indological publisher Motilal Banarsidass brought out an Indian edition that has gone through several printings.

I was invited to speak at many different venues that included colleges and universities and museums. I also gave public lectures and went on an India lecture tour that took me to Mumbai, Nagpur, Vishakhapatnam, Vijayawada, Hyderabad, Bengaluru, Thiruvananthapuram, and Chennai. In these travels, I got to personally know many of the leading intellectuals of India.

My new book, *The Gods Within,* looked at the Vedic system from the perspective of neuroscience; it argued that the Vedic gods represent elements of the structure of consciousness. This was an attempt to build bridges with the world of science.

I also did a translation of the great Kashmir Śaivism classic the Śiva Sūtra. Its very first sutra asserts that consciousness is the self, which is a most liberating idea. It makes it possible to connect the spiritual experience to science, suggesting that there are two ways to consider reality which may be seen in a unified way from another perspective.

Another sutra presents an idea that complements māyā. Just as the power of māyā is to put a covering on transcendent reality, the matṛkās, the womb of Sanskrit letters, do the opposite task of unveiling. The idea is that sound and words — as inner experience or science — can lead to the opening of the inner doorways of perception and cognition.

As creators of meaning, the matṛkās are visualized as goddesses. The Ṛgveda speaks of seven mothers who oversee the preparation of Soma and there is a famous Harappan seal which shows seven women who are presumably goddesses. Classical temples have many instances of sapta-matṛkā carvings. The Devi-Māhātmya adds one more to the list and thus speaks of aṣṭa-matṛkā.

One of the central doctrines of Kashmir Śaivism is that of recognition (*pratyabhijña*), where one's conditioned mind is able to recognize the unveiled Self. I don't see any fundamental difference between this and Advaita Vedanta for both consider universal consciousness to be the primary element of reality. If there is a difference, it is that Kashmir Śaivism takes physical reality as an embodiment of the Self whereas Advaita takes the phenomenal world to be the working of māyā, the veil of illusion. But since the cover of māyā makes the causal world emerge out of the transcendent, it is equivalent to an embodiment of the self.

The difference between Kashmir Śaivism and Advaita Vedanta is aesthetic more than anything else. If there is a tendency in Kashmir Śaivism to embrace life and beauty, in Advaita Vedanta the corresponding tendency is that of renunciation.

141

I have mentioned the Vedanta Congresses organized by Professor Rama Rao Pappu in Oxford, Ohio. Not only was this a great place to meet academic philosophers interested in India, but also those who worked at the intersection of science, society, religion, and philosophy.

Frequent participants to this congress, many of whom became good friends, included Seshagiri Rao of the University of Virginia, R. Puligandla of the University of Toledo, Arvind Sharma of McGill, T.S. Rukmini of Concordia, Ashok Aklujkar of the University of British Columbia, K.R. Sundararajan of St. Bonaventure University in New York, Stephen Phillips of the University of Texas at Austin, and Varadaraja Raman of Rochester Institute of Technology.

The idea of an Encyclopedia of Hinduism was conceived by Swami Chidananda Saraswati of the Parmarth Niketan at the Hindu-Jain Temple in Pittsburgh, Pennsylvania, in 1987. Subsequently, in November of the same year, the India Heritage Research Foundation was formed to execute the idea and K. L. Seshagiri Rao was appointed chief editor. The offices of the Encyclopedia project were established at the University of South Carolina at Columbia.

By the mid-1990s, the sheer volume of articles from all over the world overwhelmed the project administration. The main problem was the need for decisive action since there were many duplicate articles, and some were of dubious quality. Someone needed to go through the material and take the hard decision of rejecting material that was not up to the mark.

Originally, individual subscriptions constituted the funding base of the project. But as the completion of the project kept getting put off, new funding dried up and Swami

Chidananda called a special meeting of six scholars to decide on the fate of the project.

The members of this group were Seshagiri Rao, Rama Rao Pappu, Varadaraja Raman, T.S. Rukmini, K.R. Sundararajan, and I. Swami Chidananda took the help of his America-born associate and assistant Bhagawati Saraswati to decide what should be done. We met in a hotel in New Jersey and after considerable discussion it was decided that we will assume the role of Associate Editors to edit the material on an expeditious basis. After editing dozens of articles in New Jersey, each of us edited several hundred more by e-mail.

After we had done this work, Swami Chidananda moved the final editing to Delhi under the charge of Kapil Kapoor, professor of English and retired rector of Jawaharlal Nehru University. The Encyclopedia finally appeared in 2012 as a 7,184 page, 11-volume publication, with full-color illustrations of temples, places, thinkers, rituals and festivals, consisting of contributions of over 2,000 scholars. The beautifully produced American edition was released in Columbia in 2013 where many of the associate editors assembled.

———

The astronomical findings of the Vedas galvanized scholars to create a new association called WAVES (World Association of Vedic Studies), with Bhu Dev Sharma, who was then with Xavier University in New Orleans, as president. Its first conference was held on October 4-6, 1996 in Atlanta, Georgia, which was inaugurated by Basdeo Pandey, prime minister of Trinidad and Tobago. Over three hundred participants from all over the world participated. The attendees included the archaeologist Braj Basi Lal, Klaus Klostermaier, David Frawley, Śiva Bajpai, and T.R.N. Rao.

143

The proceedings of the conference received wide dissemination through television and internet. Many subsequent conferences have been held, both in the West as well as in India. But the association has not lived up to its initial promise since it was unable to carve out a proper niche to bridge the divide between academics and laypersons.

One of the television teams in Atlanta was the public television channel OHM from the Netherlands. A few years later the channel sent a team to Baton Rouge to interview me for a documentary on my work. Later on Naumi and I were invited to Amsterdam for further interviews and the channel arranged for the recreation of the Vedic fire ritual in a forest that was broadcast in due course.

17. ARCHITECTURE AND MUSIC

My research on the Agnicayana rite led to the Aśvamedha, and I wrote a book in which I explained the logic of the famous rite and used that to speak of ritual in general. Most people do not realize that ritual means different things to different people. There are two broad interpretations: literal and symbolic, and the "animals" for sacrifice can belong to either category.

The literal interpretation is the asuric interpretation whereas the deeper and inner interpretation is daivika. Over centuries, the literal interpretation has become the standard in certain communities, and many of the schisms in society are to be traced to disputes over the interpretation.

I established these points by going back to the Vedic texts and also showing the surprising ways in which the Aśvamedha ritual has similarities to the Agnicayana ritual. I also translated some of the Ṛgvedic sūktas as well as the Garbha Upaniṣad.

Some believe that the temple is a late innovation less than 2,000 years old and the representation of divinity in image form is also correspondingly late. But Indian architecture has continuity with the Harappan period, and the Agnicayana ritual uses the golden image of puruṣa. This rite is a precursor to temple ritual and the altars are a model for temple design.

The scholars Ananda Coomaraswamy and Louis Renou wrote influential papers on textual sources for architectural forms and iconography of the period starting with the Mauryas. I had long been inspired by Coomaraswamy's brilliant book of essays titled *The Dance of Śiva* and read his several other books on art and religion. The work of Renou was less accessible, since he wrote in French, but he was an influential Indologist of the twentieth century. While their general work was of importance, it appeared to me that both these scholars went astray in the assessment of Vedic architecture.

Both Coomaraswamy and Renou started with the assumption that the beginnings of Indian architecture are to be traced to the early Sūtra texts that speak of primitive structures. This assumption is wrong since earlier texts have references to palaces and cities and so the ritual structure, which may just be a flimsy shed, cannot be taken to represent the Vedic house.

Renou failed to address the question of why would a people not use bricks in the construction of the house when the same bricks are an important part of their lives in the ritual. Some people even assigned a time to this ritual when use of brick houses was common!

From temple design and its astronomical orientation (the field of archaeoastronomy) I was led to other problems of representation in sacred art. Amongst other things, I explained the count of 224 for the perwara shrines in the great temple at Prambanan in Java.

———

On one of our visits to Curtin University in Australia in 2014, we flew from Frankfurt to Perth with a layover of nearly twelve hours in Hong Kong. Arriving early morning, we had a full day ahead for sightseeing. After inquiries at the airport we chose to visit the Po Lin Monastery (Precious Lotus Zen Temple) and the Big Buddha at Ngong Ping on Lantau Island.

It was Naumi's birthday and she felt that the visit to the monastery would make the day memorable.

From the airport we took a bus to the Tung Chung Station. We were too early for the Cable Car to Ngong Ping. After what appeared to be an interminable wait, we got into a crowded bus of what appeared to be peasants. Going through villages along a circuitous route, at last we reached the high ground where the village is located. We were among the first visitors to arrive at the Po Lin Monastery.

The Monastery was established over a hundred years ago and it has grown to have many pagodas and halls that are beautifully decorated inside with extravagantly painted ceilings and colorfully rendered carved eaves. The Monastery has a set of Tripiṭaka volumes that were wood block-printed in Qing Dynasty between 1735 and 1738, and are the last official version printed in China. It also has relics of the Buddha that were brought from Sri Lanka in 1992.

Its main temple houses three bronze statues of Bhaiṣajyaguru Buddha (left), Śākyamuni Buddha (center), and Amitābha Buddha (right). Śākyamuni in the middle is attended to by the smaller images of two acolytes: the aged and austere Mahākaśyapa and the young and learned Ānanda.

The Buddhas, apart from the historical Śākyamuni (Siddhārtha Gautama), are idealized enlightened beings (bodhisattvas) who lived before and will come in the future, and Dīpaṃkara and Maitreya represent the Buddha's past and future lives; Bhaiṣajyaguru is the Buddha of healing who is popular in the East and known as Sman-bla-rgyal-po in Tibet, Yaoshi fo in China, Yakushi Nyorai in Japan, and Amitābha is the Buddha of infinite light and life. The many Buddhas and Bodhisattvas symbolize the different facets through which the mind can be apprehended.

At the lower level to the main temple is a hall that enshrines the bodhisattvas Avalokiteśvara (compassion), Mañjuśrī (insight), and Samantabhadra (worthiness). Avalokiteśvara also appears sometimes as Guanyin, the Goddess of Mercy. Most ceremonies are held in this lower hall. There is a separate shrine to the valiant general Skanda who sits behind the jovial Maitreya of the future. Another shrine is dedicated to Avalokiteśvara.

Behind the main temple is the Grand Hall of Ten Thousand Buddhas. Its lower floor has five Dhyāni Buddha ("mind-arising Buddha") statues of Amoghasidhi, Amitābha, Vairocana, Ratnasambhava and Akṣobhya, ten thousand miniature Buddha statues lining the walls and an elaborately decorated ceiling.

The fame of the Po Lin Monastery spread when the 34-meter tall Tian Tan Buddha statue was consecrated on 29 December 1993 on the anniversary of the Buddha's enlightenment. The Śākyamuni Buddha sits cross-legged on a lotus flower and faces north to look over the Chinese people. The statue's base is modeled after the Altar of Heaven of the Tian Tan — the Temple of Heaven — in Beijing.

To reach the Buddha one needs to climb 268 steps. Facing it are six smaller bronze statues of perfections (*pāramitās*) who offer flowers, incense, lamp, ointment, fruit, and music to the Buddha. These symbolize the six perfections of generosity (*dāna*), morality (*śīla*), patience (*kṣānti*), zeal (*vīrya*), meditation (*dhyāna*), and wisdom (*prajñā*).

The Buddha statue, which was constructed from 202 bronze pieces, took twelve years to complete. The Buddha's right hand is raised in the mudra of fearlessness and compassion (*abhayamudrā*) while the left rests open on his lap in a gesture of wish-fulfilment (*varadamudrā*). His palms and the sole of the foot have the imprint of the dharma-wheel, and his chest is marked by the svastika sign of auspiciousness.

Beneath the base of the statue are three additional floors: the Hall of the Universe, the Hall of Benevolent Merit, and the Hall of Remembrance. The museum has a huge carved bell inscribed with images of Buddhas. It is designed to ring at regular intervals for a total of 108 times a day, symbolizing the clearing of 108 kinds of human vexations. I explained earlier how the number 108 and other abstractions occur commonly in the Vedic tradition.

The Piazza at Ngong Ping has a Bodhi Path flanked by twelve yakṣas, also called divine generals, who are the protective deities of Bhaiṣajyaguru. Buddhists connect these generals with the 12 hours of the day and the 12 years of the calendar cycle. The yakṣa (with yakṣī or yakṣiṇī) is the archetype custodian of treasures and the principal among them is Kubera, who rules the mythical Himalayan kingdom called Alakā. In Kashmir, yakṣa-amāvasya was a popular festival on the new moon's day in the winter month of Pauṣa (December/January). A plate with fish, lentils and other dishes was left out in the courtyard at night for the yakṣa.

Those born under different zodiac signs are taken to be protected by eight different deities. The visit to the monastery was most rewarding. We had seen much of the ideals or archetypes of the psyche that are at the basis of the practice of religion in East and Southeast Asia.

We lit incense sticks in front of the monastery before returning to the airport to catch our flight. The monastery in the outskirts of this great metropolis of the east had opened a window to a world of abstractions in Sanskrit that we only knew at a visceral level.

I had long wished to see the temples of Java and Bali. We flew to Bali from Perth. Since Bali is closer to Perth than any other large city in Australia, it is a popular vacation destination for Western Australians. From Bali we flew to Yogyakarta one early morning to see Borobudur and Prambanan and returned late at night.

Bali is a paradise for artists, tourists, surfers, partiers, and art buyers. The new airport at Denpasar is attractive but the general feel on the road and walking in the streets is quite similar to that in India. We stayed in a traditional hotel in Seminyak, not far from the beach, which had rooms that looked like villas.

Literally, every other shop near the beach is a spa, with rates perhaps one-tenth of those in Western cities. Many of the art studios are located in the central Bali town of Ubud, which is not far away from its volcanoes, the monkey-forest, and stunning rice terraces overlooked by charming restaurants.

The first day trip out of our hotel in Seminyak included a Barong dance show that gave us a clue to the Balinese aesthetic. The show has some pleasing elements and great costumes. We were to later see a Kecaka Ramayana performance at the Ulu Watu temple complex on the cliffs in South Bali. We visited the Tirtha Empul Temple which has a spring whose waters are said to wash away one's sins, and also saw the stunning complex of temples at Tanah Lot including the Śiva temple that gets cut off at high tide. Bali and Java are great for jewelry, wooden crafts, batik and art.

––––––––––

Bhinneka Tunggal Ika, the national motto of Indonesia, literally means "different, yet the same." Since this sounds paradoxical, it is usually rendered as "unity in diversity." The phrase is from the *Kakawin Sutosoma*, a fourteenth century poem in Old Javanese, by Mpu Tantular.

The context for this phrase is the centuries-old competition in Java between the traditions of the Veda (as in the worship of Śiva, who symbolizes universal consciousness) and the Buddha, whose followers believe that beyond the mind is emptiness. Two royal families ruled different kingdoms in this area: the Sanjaya was devoted to Śiva while the Shailendra worshiped the Buddha. The two dynasties built great temples of which the most famous are the Candi Prambanan and the Candi Borobudur, both in the vicinity of Yogyakarta. To explain the terminology, an old temple in Indonesia is called *candi*, suggesting that the earliest temples in Java were dedicated to Durga's fierce form and then the name became generic, whereas newer functioning temples are called *pura*.

Yogyakarta (Skt. *yogya* meaning "fit" and *karta* meaning "established," or "prosperous city"), in Central Java, is the city of Indonesian high culture which is also a center for arts and crafts and wayang (shadow puppet theatre). The ninth century Prambanan temple complex is 17 kilometers in the northeast direction of Yogyakarta and due south of Mount Merapi.

The temple is primarily to Śiva, with subsidiary temples to Vishnu and Brahma. It is famous for the image of Durga, known locally as Loro Jonggrang (Slender Virgin), and the temple is also known as Candi Loro Jonggrang. Rakai Pikatan, the Sanjaya King, who is credited with the building of Prambanan, also built the beautiful Buddhist Plaosan temple for his wife, Pramodhawardhani, the daughter of the Shailendra king Samaratunga. Thus the kings recognized that behind the difference between the two traditions was the same truth.

151

The Borobudur complex, also from the ninth century, is the world's largest Buddhist temple that covers an entire hill as a pyramid. Approximately 40 kilometers northwest of Yogyakarta, it is located in an elevated area that stretches to volcanoes on two sides. Two other temples, Pawon and Mendut, lie on the line with Mount Merapi, highlighting its special place in a sacred landscape. Ascending from the base of the monument one passes through three levels of Buddhist cosmology: Kāmadhātu (the realm of desire), Rūpadhātu (the realm of forms) and Arūpyadhātu (the world of formlessness). Kāmadhātu is represented by the base, Rūpadhātu by the five square platforms (the body), and Arūpyadhātu by the three circular platforms and the large topmost stupa.

We also visited the Sultan's palace, the Kraton, which was built in 1755. Even though built by a Muslim Sultan, it has its own sacred landscape which parallels that of Borbudur. Stretching from Mount Merapi is a straight line that passes through the unity monument of Tugu Yogyakarta, the Kraton, and Panggung Krapyak where the Sultans hunted, which forms a sacred north-south axis to the Southern Ocean. The continuity across the traditions is further seen in craft of the puppets and the wayang performance.

Let me now turn to the Kakawin Sutosoma for the phrase *Bhinneka Tunggal Ika*. The stanza is as follows:

Rwāneka dhātu winuwus Buddha Wiswa,
Bhinnêki rakwa ring apan kena parwanosen,
Mangka ng Jinatwa kalawan Śiwatatwa tunggal,
Bhinnêka tunggal ika tan hana dharma mangrwa.

The Buddha and the Universal (Śiva) are known as different realms

They are different, but how to know this difference
For the truth of Jina (Buddha) and Śiva is one
They are different, yet same, for truth knows no
duality.

The stanza speaks of the realms of the Buddha and the Vishva (the universal consciousness as Śiva) and says that they are different, yet the same. What are the realms that appear different? The Buddha realm is the realm of intelligence and thought, whereas the realm of Śiva is that of pure awareness. They are the same if you believe (with the Buddhists) that beyond the mind lies śūnyatā (emptiness) and they appear to be different if you think that beyond the mind is the transcendent reality of ātman or Īśvara. But since you cannot approach pure awareness with thought, the difference has little influence on practice.

By saying *Bhinneka Tunggal Ika*, Mpu Tantular made a subtle point about belief. The words, buddhi and consciousness, that are used by the Buddhists and the Hindus to indicate the ultimate nature of reality may be different in abstract terms, but from a practical point of view, the two paths are nearly identical.

In my Vedic studies I had come across a fascinating book titled *The Myth of Invariance* by Ernest McClain. This book presented an explanation of certain parts of Vedic mythology in musicological terms although its main emphasis was on Greek and Babylonian themes. In some ways, it echoed the Chāndogya Upaniṣad about connections between meters and myth that I had myself used in the analysis of the Aśvamedha rite. The book had other elements that I was not in a position to judge. I felt McClain's idea that ancient tales and myths

153

preserved and conveyed real numerical information about musical tuning could not be the whole story and there were aspects that needed further investigation.

I was surprised when I received a letter from McClain inviting me to take his ideas further and use them for a deeper examination of Indian texts. I responded that I lacked knowledge of musicology but he pressed on, writing dozens of beautifully crafted long letters exhorting me to rise to the challenge. These letters, which could very well be bound together into a book, were inspiring but all I could do was to put him off.

McClain had been connected to the musicologist Siegmund Levarie and the pianist and composer Ernst Levy from whom he learnt of Albert von Thimus' Pythagoreanism which became his key to unlocking Plato's mathematical and musical riddles. He had also collaborated with the philosopher Antonio de Nicolas whose book *Meditations Through the Ṛgveda* I had read. Antonio de Nicolas also wrote to me encouraging me to investigate musical tuning and myth. McClain remained a frequent correspondent until he died at the age of 94 in 2014.

In late 2001 I received an e-mail for José Maceda inviting me to a conference on musicology in Manila in late February 2002 with the theme *A Search in Asia for a New Theory of Music*. I was surprised at the invitation for in spite of my long correspondence with McClain; I did not have the expertise to speak on music.

Researching Maceda on the Internet, I discovered that he was a professor, composer, professional pianist and a living treasure of the Philippines. He studied piano with Alfred Cortot in Paris during late 1930s and later with Robert Schmitz in the USA before training in musique concrète composition in Paris in 1958. After a doctorate in ethnomusicology from the UCLA in 1963, he taught at the

University of the Philippines for many years. He had known and promoted Pierre Boulez, Karlheinz Stockhausen, Iannis Xenakis and other composers. A National Artist for Music in the Philippines, he was born the same year as my father.

I wrote to him asking if he was sure he wanted me to come to the conference and he said yes and the reason he had chosen me was my knowledge of the Veda. He explained that the symposium was for finding a rapprochement between the musics of Asia and Europe for the aesthetics of the two were different. He felt that this coming together could be similar to the Italian Renaissance that created a new synthesis of music in Europe. He spoke of four foundational ideas: relationship of music and cosmology, mathematical structures underlying the court musics of East and Southeast Asia, the relationship between languages and music, and finally the nature of music and social organization. He thought something overarching like the connections between cosmology and meters that I had discovered could provide the key to the solution.

I had just a few months to learn ethnomusicology in a systematic way. The weeklong conference, organized by the Center for Ethnomusicology at the University of the Philippines, was wonderfully planned and Maceda was a superb host. He looked and acted decades younger than his age of eighty-five and I was gratified that he took time out to speak to me at length.

The participant from India was my friend Kapila Vatsyayan, the pre-eminent historian of the arts in India. In her presentation, Kapilaji highlighted the fundamental nature of the square, the circle, and the triangle in artistic structures. She also spoke of how rasa, as a theory of aesthetics, permeates the domains of architecture, sculpture, painting, poetry, drama, music and dance. My own paper was on early music where I described the connections between

155

Vedic chanting with its three notes, the seven notes of the octave, and the 22 śrutis or microtones of Indian music. There was much about music and the arts that I learnt from Kapilaji and Jose Maceda on this trip.

The musicologists at the conference invited me to a meeting the following year in Busan, Korea, to speak on the Indian epic song tradition, where I spoke of medieval and more recent epic song cycles of north and south India.

One thing leads to another. A few years later, I heard from the film producer Gita Desai, who had a few years earlier interviewed me for a movie called *Yoga Unveiled*. She now wished to interview me for a new documentary on Hindustani Classical Music in which she was being advised by Vijay Kichlu, a well-known vocalist who had for many years served as director of the ITC Music Academy in Kolkata. She had already traveled the world over to interview the foremost performers and musicologists.

My part of the filming was done in Connecticut where Gita then lived, and the documentary was eventually released with the title *Raga Unveiled*. Gita used my part of the interview as introduction to different segments to narrate the larger story of Indian classical music.

18. THE TWIN PARADOX AND NONLOCALITY

The problem of time has intrigued philosophers and physicists for hundreds of years, and it was one of my concerns in my book on the nature of physical reality. Newton famously considered space and time to be absolute until relativity theory showed he was wrong since time flows at different rates for different observers in different states of motion. But what if two observers were to start at the same place, experience time differently due to different motions and then come together?

This problem had been partly anticipated by the authors of the Purāṇas as in this well-known passage in the Bhāgavata Purāṇa: "Taking his own daughter, Revati, Kakudmi went to Brahmā in Brahmaloka, and inquired about a husband for her. When Kakudmi arrived there, Brahmā was engaged in hearing musical performances by the Gandharvas and had not a moment to talk with him. Therefore Kakudmi waited, and at the end of the performance he saluted Brahmā and made his desire known. After hearing his words, Brahmā laughed loudly and said to Kakudmi, 'O King, all those whom you may have decided within the core of your heart to accept as your son-in-law have passed away in the course of time. Twenty-seven caturyugas have already passed. Those upon whom you may have decided are now gone, and so are their sons, grandsons and other descendants. You cannot even hear about their names.'" But there is no paradox in this story since the narrative clearly specifies which party is aging faster.

The general Indian ideas on time were summarized by Al-Bīrūnī in his classic history of India written in 1032 CE: "The Hindus have divided duration into two periods, a period of motion, which has been determined as time, and a period of rest, which can only be determined in an imaginary way according to the analogy of that which has first been determined, the period of motion. The Hindus hold the eternity of the Creator to be determinable, not measurable, since it is infinite... They do not, by the word creation, understand a formation of something out of nothing. They mean by creation only the working with a piece of clay, working out various combinations and figures in it, and making such arrangements with it as will lead to certain ends and aims which are potentially in it." Time was thus seen as emerging out of motion and not something absolute. Implicit in this view is that the evolution of the universe is consistent although the experience of time may vary for different individuals.

The idea of phenomena being independent of motion of certain kind was advanced by the astronomers Āryabhaṭa and Galileo. The formal theory of relativity that emerged out of the work of Poincare, Einstein and others considers all frames moving at uniform speed to be equivalent. A body moving at uniform speed does so due to inertia, and such frames are called inertial. According to this theory, time flows with different rates if the frames are moving with respect to each other. This does not lead to a problem when the frames are moving away and the elapsed times cannot be compared. But what if the frames are brought together? If that is done, it leads to the twin paradox that was first pointed out by Paul Langevin in 1911.

According to relativity theory the speed of light is the same for all observers. This is counterintuitive because normally, in the classical world, speed is additive. In relativity, the constancy of the speed of light is maintained by the contraction or lengthening of measuring rods and related change in the rate at which clocks move. This means that space and time in themselves cannot be considered absolute.

If a twin took off on a fast spaceship, he will, on his return, find the earthbound twin to have aged considerably more due to the slowing down of moving clocks compared to stationary clocks. For example, if the spaceship went to the nearest star 4.45 light years away at 86% of the speed of light, when it returns the traveling twinhas aged 5 years whereas the earthbound twin has aged over 10 years.

Paul Langevin gave a more striking example by describing a traveler making a trip at 99.995% the speed of light. He travels out for one year of his time, and then reverses direction. Upon return, he finds that he has aged two years, while 200 years have passed on Earth.

The slowing down of time on moving objects has been confirmed in physical experiments. The paradox is that with respect to the twin on the spaceship it is the earthbound twin who is in motion and, therefore, he should be younger. Many solutions have been proposed for the paradox but they are inconsistent with each other.

Some resolutions ignore the fact that the Earth itself is not in uniform motion, for it moves around the Sun, which, in turn, moves in the galaxy, and so on, and there is a further accelerating expansion of the universe. Other resolutions privilege one frame against another, making assumptions that go beyond the statement of the paradox.

———

The treatment of a paradox is an excellent place to find out about the underlying philosophical problem. It may be argued that a formal system is unable to prove what lies beyond its framework and scientific theory does not provide unrestricted inferences in the system.

There is the complementary issue of the relationship between theory and physical reality, and here the question of what constitutes information is open to interpretation. If a theory has no terms to describe a specific phenomenon, that phenomenon would simply not exist within it and in corresponding descriptions of physical reality.

The underlying philosophical position might be to take laws to be independent of the universe, or it may assume that the laws must, in some sense, be reflective of the nature of the universe. The treatment may turn on the amount and nature of information that the frames have, or it may overlook this information altogether.

The twin paradox appears puzzling because each twin sees the other twin as moving, and so, according to a naïve application of time dilation and the principle of relativity, each should paradoxically find the other to have aged more slowly.

Max von Laue argued in 1913 that since the traveling twin must be in two separate inertial frames, one on the way out and another on the way back, this frame switch is the reason for the aging difference, and not the acceleration per se, for the time of acceleration can be made arbitrarily small compared with the time of inertial motion. But if the traveling twin spends an overwhelming part of his travel in uniform motion, why should his clock move slowly just because of the acceleration event?

On the other hand, Albert Einstein and Max Born argued that gravitational time dilation was the explanation for the aging and it was a direct effect of acceleration.

In a paper published in 2007, I proposed a solution based on a new way of looking at the problem that allows one to see unambiguously which of the two twins is in motion. In this resolution the speed of the twin is measured in relation to that of the rest of the universe.

My solution identifies inertial frames unambiguously by considered global information, which is not possible by considering only a local region. The traveler who moves with respect to the ambient conditions of the universe will be younger and one cannot speak of the motion of the two twins in isolation.

———

If nonlocality is central to relativity, it is so to quantum theory as well. When two particles are entangled then their properties, although random in principle, remain connected even if the particles were to be billions of miles apart and there is no way the measurement on one could be relayed to the other.

Suppose the entangled particles are electrons, with spins in opposite directions. Further assume that two distantly located parties have used prior synchronization to fix their orientations and also agreed on which directions to make the measurements. If one party obtains up-spin, the second party will obtain down-spin and vice versa. This implies that reality is nonlocal.

Modern physics considers information in many different ways and it is generally done in the garb of entropy, which represents average information. This raises the question as to who is processing the information. Some suggest that physics deals with the nature of the mind, for it is in the mind that theories are conceived and tested. Information resides in collectives and not isolated objects; therefore we must assume that the observer has the capacity to make intelligent classifications and choices, either directly or through the agency of instruments and computing devices.

From this perspective also, use of information is an implicit acknowledgement of mind.

In 2005, Hurricane Katrina devastated New Orleans and other parts of Louisiana. Both our children had studied in that city: Abhinav was at the Medical School and Arushi had spent a year as undergraduate at Tulane University. Large parts of the city that are below the sea level were drowned when the embankments broke.

Many people were able to escape although it took them the whole day to drive sixty miles to Baton Rouge; others were trapped in houses and there was much confusion and looting, reports of murder and rape, and nearly 1,500 deaths. Those who could not leave were housed in the Superdome at the edge of the city and this became the focus of the media.

Once the Superdome refugees were found temporary accommodations elsewhere, police cordoned off the city and no one was allowed to enter for several months. After about three months, Abhinav and I sneaked in. The water in the submerged areas had dried out and the city presented a surreal look like an abandoned city in war or a city hit by a neutron bomb that killed all life but spared the buildings.

Reaching Abhinav's apartment, which was on high ground and had stayed safe, we gathered the most significant valuables in the car to take home. Later Abhinav and his friends rented a truck to get other belongings out.

Abhinav's medical school set up a temporary campus in Baton Rouge and Arushi transferred to LSU. The economy of the State of Louisiana was in dire straits and the following year I decided to look around for a position in another state.

I was invited to visit several campuses and accepted an offer from Oklahoma State University Stillwater to be the head of the computer science department.

———

Before I could join my new position in Oklahoma, Naumi and I were invited to visit Mysore, where I was to be awarded the title of *Vishwa Hindu* by Sri Ganapati Sachchidananda Swami, the spiritual head of Avadhoota Datta Peetham, a major center for Vedic studies and spiritual life. The date chosen for the award, May 20, 2007, was also the celebration of Swamiji's sixty-fifth birthday and the Brahmotsavam of Sri Datta Venkateshwara Temple.

Swamiji is not only a spiritual teacher but also a masterful musician. He has travelled extensively around the world to spread spiritual knowledge and healing through music that he calls rāgarāginī vidyā.

Datta Peetham is situated on a lovely forty-acre site at the foot of Chamundi Hill in Mysore, and it looks and feels like a little city. This is the world headquarters of Swamiji's mission, with centers in many countries. It is a place for both the aspirant and the scholar and one can study yoga, the Vedas, the Āgamas, Sanskrit, ritual and music. The Peetham has a prayer hall where traditional pujas and homas are performed, and a magnificent auditorium.

We flew in to Bengaluru arriving at midnight and a waiting SUV brought us to the ashram in Mysore. For the celebrations, nearly twenty-thousand people from all over the world and the elite from Bengaluru had gathered. There were aspirants eager for spiritual knowledge but also others who helped Swamiji with running the activities of the ashram. Amongst these latter was K.V. Krishna Murty, the head of I-SERVE, Institute of Scientific Research on Vedas, who was keen to translate some of my works into Telugu.

We were part of many ceremonies during the day and in the evening the Vishwa Hindu award was presented by Swamiji in the huge amphitheater-like-auditorium. A few other awards were also presented.

The next morning, Swamiji sent word asking me to speak to the entire congregation, giving me just a few minutes to collect my thoughts. I spoke for about forty minutes on aparā and parā vidyā of the Vedas, the centrality of ṛta or natural law, the achievements of modern science and its inability to explain consciousness. I told a lot of stories and the huge audience seemed to like it. After I had finished, Swamiji paraphrased my speech into Telugu and Kannada.

Later we walked part of the 1,008 steps to the top of Chamundi Hill. Sri Radhakrishna, our guide from the ashram, facilitated the darshan of Goddess Chamundi at the Cāmuṇḍeśvari Temple in the presence of huge crowds who had assembled there for a festival. Later we sat in the hallways of the Mahābaleshvara Temple, which was very quiet on this occasion, and Radhakrishna sang beautiful devotional stotras.

Returning to Bengaluru, we visited Halebidu, Belur and other marvels of Hoysala architecture. We also saw the 57-foot tall monolithic statue of Gommateshvara (Bāhubalī) on the Vindhyāgiri Hill at Śravaṇabeḷagoḷa. Emperor Chandragupta Maurya is said to have died there in 298 BCE.

19. Oklahoma

I joined my new job at Stillwater in July 2007, and Naumi was to join me after the Baton Rouge house was sold. We had bought a condominium for Abhinav and Arushi not far from home and so the sale of the house was not going to impact them.

The dean of the College of Arts and Sciences at OSU was Peter Sherwood, an Englishman whose family had connections with India that went back a couple of centuries. He had done his Ph.D. in chemistry from Cambridge, subsequently taught in Britain and Kansas State University, and served a stint as program manager at the National Science Foundation before accepting the deanship at Oklahoma State. We developed rapport quite readily and he told me that he would support me in whichever way I thought was best for the department.

For the first three months I stayed in an apartment on the OSU campus. Mother came to be with me for a month. Her lungs were in bad shape and she could walk only slowly so I thought it would be great for her health if we took walks every morning. Before the break of dawn we would set out for an hour-long walk through a beautiful trail on high ground which was also used by the boys and girls of the university track team. Most of these mornings, we were joined by Krushna Patil, an agricultural engineer at OSU. These were delightful walks, as if transported to the magical time of my childhood walking with mother excepting that I wasn't a child any more. She was invited to give a speech at a public meeting that I think was the first and only public speech she gave in America.

Naumi was able to sell the house in three months. After she came to Stillwater, we lived for a year in a rented place and the following year we bought our own house.

Stillwater is a lovely little college town of about fifty thousand which is an hour away from the large cities of Tulsa and Oklahoma City. My immunologist cousin Rashmi and her physician husband Anil Kaul lived in Tulsa and worked for the Center of Health Science of OSU. Their presence so near Stillwater had been a factor in my accepting this job.

The OSU campus is attractive, if a bit staid and conservative in its architecture. Up the hill, beyond married student housing, students can rent small patches of vegetable garden for ten or fifteen dollars a semester.

Soon we got to know a large number of people in both Tulsa and Oklahoma City. Amongst these was Pramode Verma, a professor in the Tulsa branch of the University of Oklahoma, in whose optical engineering laboratory we decided to implement a new quantum cryptography protocol I had proposed a few years earlier. The National Science Foundation agreed to fund this research.

I also met with the local industry leaders to explore avenues for collaborative research, and helped a local utilities company in developing its web presence.

Since my academic position at OSU had an administrative component, I had to attend many meetings. I took to the administrative role well for I was happy to delegate much of the responsibility to committees and colleagues. Nevertheless, personnel matters and resolution of disputes between individuals took time.

Unlike my research in Baton Rouge that had covered different areas of engineering and physics, I now focused on mainstream theoretical computer science. Advising students and reviewing their work required much discussion.

Lectures took us to India as well as Peru, South Africa, Australia, Czech Republic, Hungary, Holland, the Caribbean, and England and at each place we made sure to do sightseeing. I remember the beauty of Cape Town and the Table Mountain and the stunning drive to the Cape of Good Hope. From Prague, another magnificent city, we took the train to Berlin to see the bust of Nefertiti in the Neues Museum and other antiquities in the Pergamon Museum. Many years ago, I had written a chapter on Akhenaten and his wives Nefertiti and Tadukhipa and investigated possible connections between his new religion and the religion of his junior wife who was a Mitanni princess.

For boldness of geography, Machu Picchu of Peru is a unique place. In the high desert on the roof of the world on the Andes, imagine the abstract geometrical structure of a bowl within a larger bowl with an axle in the middle. The axle is the mountain called Putucusi that juts up next to the river Urubamba (also called Vilcanota) surrounded by four mountains in a circle on the crest of one of which is the medieval astronomical observatory of Machu Picchu. Around these mountains lies another ring of mountains.

> *From air to air, like an empty net*
> *I went between the streets and atmosphere*
> *arriving and departing...*
> – Pablo Neruda in The Heights of Machu Picchu

The Pachu Picchu site is at the end of the Sacred Valley of the Incas that was seen to mirror the Milky Way. The sanctuary of Machu Picchu itself has temples, an upper town and a lower town. It also has a tower that was used as observatory and a ritual stone that is illuminated directly on the winter solstice. The buildings atop Machu Picchu are arranged in the forms of a flying lizard on one side and a puma on the other.

For those who find mathematical abstractions pointless, the charming village of Aguas Calientes (Hot Springs) at the base of the Central Mountain and hikes on the Inca Trail and the many archaeological sites such as Pisac and Ollantaytambo in the Sacred Valley are sufficient diversions. A bit further off is the Inca Imperial Capital of Cusco which the Incans considered the centre of the earth.

Naumi and I flew into Lima, savored its sights and antiquities, and then took another flight to Cusco atthe elevation of nearly 12,000 feet. The elevation didn't seem to bother me perhaps because of my childhood in Leh, which has nearly the same elevation. Cusco airport has oxygen booths for those experiencing breathing problems. The Andean people themselves have chewed on coca leaves to alleviate altitude sickness, fatigue, and even hunger. We were served coca tea in the plane and it was freely served in the hotels but I did not like its taste.

There are striking parallels between the cosmologies of the Inca and the Indians. Like Viṣṇu or Śiva, the Peruvians saw the Great God Viracocha of the Inca pantheon as the creator of all things. In one legend he fathers one son, Inti (Sun), and two daughters, Mama Killa (Moon) and Pachamama (Earth). The Vedas somewhat similarly divide the universe into the three regions of the heavens (symbolized variously by Sūrya, Śiva, Viṣṇu together with their mounts horse, bull, and eagle, respectively) the atmosphere (ruled by Vāyu or Indra with their mounts of gazelle and elephant), and the earth (ruled by Agni who rides the ram). The Inca cosmos has three levels of Hanan Pacha, the sky (for the gods and symbolized by the condor), Kay Pacha the earth (for the humans, symbolized by the puma), and Uku Pacha the underground (for the dead and the new stirrings of life, symbolized by the snake). The symbols of condor, puma, and the snake and the Inca cross are pervasive in Inca art and architecture.

The deeper parallel between the Inca and the Vedic beliefs is in the mapping of the outer and the inner. The Indian temple or the city symbolically represents the universe; the city of Cusco is in the shape of a puma. The cathedral where the imperial palace stood was the heart, Qurikancha the temple of the sun was the genitalia of the puma, and Saksaywaman was the head. According to ancient chronicles Qurikancha featured a large solid golden disc studded with precious stones that represented Inti. Saksaywaman was a walled complex in the north made of immense boulders where the annual Inca festival of the winter solstice and New Year is celebrated.

———

In Portugal, I was to give a lecture on science and religion at the city hall in the town of Barcelos, north of Porto. I spoke on the connections between Vedanta and quantum mechanics and how this had something to do with unfolding developments in consciousness research.

This was a series in which the first speaker was Mario Soares who had served as prime minister and president of Portugal. Our hosts were the businesswoman Rita Andrade de Almeida and her husband Antonio Cunha, a prominent lawyer. They put us up in one wing of their wonderful house and we spent a magnificent week with them and their friends.

The next year, there was much talk in the New Age Movement of the prophecy of the beginning of a new era in December 2012, and it so happened that we were at a conference in London around this time. On a beautiful snowy day on 12 December we took a day trip to Stonehenge, which is situated on the broad Salisbury Chalk Plain. By the time we arrived, the snow had stopped and we circumambulated the monument with Druids who were going clockwise as against the anti-clockwise that the tourists were advised. We were there at noon and it was only later we recognized the numerical symmetry of our time at the monument, that is 12:12:12 on 12-12-12.

In India, I visited the Dayalbagh Educational Institute (DEI) on several occasions to give talks on quantum computing, philosophy and spirituality. It was inspiring to see people live by the precept of simple living and high thinking. The spiritual head of the Radhasoami community, Prem Saran Satsangi, was an old colleague of mine from the IIT days. He did his Ph.D. in Canada on systems science applied to transportation. He was a member of the Radhasoami community even in the 1970s, but now he had come to formally lead it.

The field of quantum computing is now a fashionable area of research. Its attraction is that if quantum computers were built, they would solve certain numerical problems faster than any classical computer. My own research has argued that such computers, while sound in theory, will never be implemented for reasons of what I call the initialization problem of quantum computing and for random errors that cannot be practically corrected.

The visit to Budapest, Hungary was at the invitation of the International Astronomical Union which was celebrating the 500th anniversary of the invention of the telescope by Galileo. The conference director was the physicist and musician Atilla Grandpierre who arranged a TV interview. As a musician he is best known as vocalist of a rock band called Galloping Coroners (Vágtázó Halottkémek in Hungarian). One of the other speakers was Menas Kafatos of Chapman University who, I was pleasantly surprised to find, has a deep interest in Kashmir Śaivism.

I was to run into Kafatos many times in the next few years. He was a speaker at the Towards a Science of Consciousness Conference that was held in Agra at DEI. Another speaker at this conference was the famed author and speaker Deepak Chopra.

Chopra, a physician, has challenged many nostrums of Western medicine by championing Āyurveda and Vedantic insights important in the process of healing. An excellent communicator of the insights of Vedanta, he has become a guru to the rich and the famous around the world.

Chopra invited me to speak at his Sages and Scientists meeting in California, which brings together leading scientists and scholars from around the world to discuss advances in the fields of consciousness science, viewed as the intersection of quantum theory, cosmology, philosophy, neuroscience, medicine, and yoga. This was a superbly organized meeting and the other speakers included the ex-president of Mexico, Vincente Fox, the author Arianna Huffington, and prominent businessmen and scientists.

Around this time, I was also asked to write an autobiographical essay on my work in a special issue on pioneers of quantum learning for a journal at the intersection of quantum theory and neuroscience. This was the draft that evolved to become the present book.

Meanwhile, Colin Ruggles, one of the world's pre-eminent archaeoastronomers was editing a book listing the world's heritage sites of archaeoastronomy for International Council on Monuments and Sites (ICOMOS). He put together a team of fifteen editors to cover the globe and he asked me to be the editor for the Indian region. This gave me the reason to write the first systematic review of archaeoastronomy in India in the volume that appeared in 2010.

I stepped down as head of the department after two three-year terms and I could now apply myself to research projects that had lain dormant for a few years. Meanwhile, Arushi got engaged to her classmate, Nivedh Paluvoi, in May 2012, and the marriage took place two years later at the Andrew W. Mellon Auditorium in Washington, DC.

20. TRINIDAD

I first went to Trinidad in August 2000 as a keynote speaker at the World Hindu Conference. It was a large meeting with over a thousand delegates. The speakers included K.S. Sudarshan, Ashok Singhal and Narendra Modi from India, Prime Minister Basdeo Panday, Sat Maharaj and Ralph Maraj from Trinidad, Swami Aksharananda from Guyana, and a host of Swamis including Swami Chidananda Saraswati of Parmarth Ashram in Haridwar. I also met brilliant intellectuals from the Caribbean.

We got to see villages outside of St. Augustine campus of the University of Trinidad and Tobago where the conference was held and I especially enjoyed giving a talk at a village temple. I also saw Siewdass Sadhu's Temple in the Sea that is a tourist attraction and has the most unlikely history.

Sadhu was born on January 1, 1903 and travelled to Trinida and Tobago with his parents and two younger brothers when he was four years old. He worked as an indentured laborer during his youth. He built a small temple in 1947 on lands owned by a sugar cane company. When his master discovered this structure, it was pulled down and he was charged with trespassing, fined and put in prison. Sadhu now resolved to build his temple in the sea beyond the jurisdiction of the sugar cane company. He used a bucket and an old lady's bicycle with a carrier at the back to transport rocks and dirt to make an artificial island in the sea that took many years and after that he built a temple on it. This temple was renovated twenty years ago.

I was impressed that Indians in Trinidad had confronted problems of modernity related to religious matters and questions of otherness due to the mingling of races much before thinkers in India had given careful thought to these problems.

In my second visit in 2010, Naumi accompanied me. This time the occasion was the WAVES (World Association of Vedic Studies) conference. Malay Mishra, who was the Indian High Commissioner in Port of Spain, asked me to address a large gathering of dignitaries that were invited to his home.

Our friends David Frawley and his wife Shambhavi and Shekhar Shastri and his wife Vanita were also there. Naumi and Vanita gave brilliant talks on their experience of Dharma in the general assembly. I saw a giant Hanuman statue at the Datta Peetham temple on the island on this trip.

In 2013, we made a short visit to Trinidad to inaugurate the Vivekananda Society of Trinidad and Tobago (VSTT). I was asked to speak on "Self Discovery through Direct Experience," whereas Naumi's speech was on "Empowerment of Women through Vedanta." The chairman of VSTT was a retired doctor named Rampersad Parasram who did his medical training in India and spoke excellent Hindi. I had heard him give a brilliant recitation of the Ramayana Katha on the earlier trip.

The idea of VSTT is to keep the message of Sri Ramakrishna and Vivekananda alive in Trinidad and do education and other volunteer projects.

My advice to VSTT was that in view of the changed world that we live in, the society should focus on the areas of science, well being (including meditation, Āyurveda, and yoga), and outreach (through socially aware projects and charity).

21. REMEMBERING MOTHER

Mother was just eighteen years older to me and I remember how she herself was growing up as I was making sense of the world. Since I was a quiet boy, she would take me along to her lady-friends in the afternoon and I sat in a corner reading a book and listened to the conversation.

Mother was generous to a fault. She protected us with fierce energy when we were young and as we grew older her prayers became our shield. She sometimes gave vent to frustration at father's unworldly ways but she also admired his calm and absolute faith that things will work out.

She lost her mother in 1950 and father in 1952. When we came to Srinagar, we stayed with her brother, Radha Krishan, and his wife, Shanta. We spent so much time there during holidays that the children, Vinay, Promila, and Rashmi, became like our siblings.

Her oldest brother, our Uncle Kashi Nath, who had lived in Delhi for many years, was in later years transferred to Srinagar. After a few years in the official residence on the Bund, he and his wife, Chand Rani, moved into the second floor of Radha Krishan's home in Jawahar Nagar and this place became a kind of a mini-family compound with relatives making social calls in the evenings.

In winter, mother sat for hours knitting sweaters or socks and humming abstract tunes that were so comforting that one still aches to hear them again. She couldn't sing but her humming was magical.

———

In June 2012, mother was hospitalized with pneumonia. She had previously been in hospital and I hoped that like before she would pull through. I spoke to her on phone in early June, before she fell ill, and told her that I had booked my ticket to visit Delhi in early August. She was quiet for a moment and then said it will be too late. She said she was old and it was time to go, but then she changed the subject.

I now heard that mother's condition was serious and we should come to Delhi immediately. Avinash and Neeraj left first and when they saw mother in the hospital she was not responsive. I left the next day arriving on the night of 10 July. Meanwhile, Jaishree, who was visiting her son Vajra in China, also tried her best to advance her trip to Delhi.

I saw mother in the hospital next morning. She was hooked to the breathing machine but was alert and her mind was clear. The doctor said that she looked so good that she would be discharged the next day. Facing her, we sat against the wall, Avinash, Neeraj, Shakti, Divya, and I. The nurse asked her to tell who was who and she pointed at each one of us correctly. When I went to the side of the bed to speak she asked me who else had come with me. Then she looked me straight in the eyes and repeated the first line of father's favorite Sanskrit hymn: *na tāto na mātā na bandhur na dātā* (there is no father, no mother, no relative, no brother with the second unsaid line stating that it is to you, O Goddess, that I offer myself). This is the hymn we had all sung together, crying, at father's funeral in Honolulu. She also said it was time to go. She said some other things also but she was speaking softly and the words became indistinct due to the breathing mask that lay over her mouth.

The doctor had said encouraging words, so we went to check out a nearby nursing home and it looked quite promising. But when we returned to the hospital in the

176

afternoon, mother's vital signs were sinking and in the hour or so we were there she was fighting for each breath, which was most painful to watch.

At 9:30 PM we received a call from the hospital asking us to return immediately and by the time we arrived she was gone and the hospital staff was giving her CPR to revive her heart, but in vain.

Jaishree and Vajra arrived the next day from China. The funeral was done on Friday. On Saturday, we went to Garh Mukteshwar to immerse the ashes in the Ganga River. It was a bright sunny day, and we rented a boat to take us midstream for the immersion. As the boat pushed off a cloud gathered in the sky and it began to rain. By the time we came back to the shore the cloud had dispersed and it was sunny again.

I returned to the United States at the end of the tenth-day ritual. I felt empty and didn't want to think what it meant. She had gone through much physical suffering in the last few years.

Now we did not have her protection. Her presence was like a big umbrella that kept us away from harsh weather. How would we all do without her presence? In a larger sense, it was as if a powerful link to India had been severed.

Mother was a remarkable person. By the force of her personality she became the exemplar for her children and relatives. She believed in working hard but did not take herself too seriously and laughed at herself easily.

She valued books and knowledge a great deal and nothing gave her as much pleasure as to see her children and grandchildren invested in learning. She was proud of the many books her children had written and pleased when father's autobiography was published posthumously. Her own book of poems *Nagar aur Vairāgya* (City and Renunciation) appeared when she turned 75.

During the 70s, I spent a few weeks every summer with my parents. I remember one memorable trip in father's jeep when we went to Reasi, where we saw the house where father had roomed as a young man and studied with his spiritual teacher Mr Kalia. My parents had been to the Vaishno Devi shrine before, so only Shakti and I set out in the evening for the cave up the mountain and were back by dawn. On this trip, we also visited the lovely towns of Kishtwar and Bhadarwah.

After father's retirement, mother's sister Aruna suggested that they should move to Delhi. Aruna and her husband Zind Lal Kaul and eldest sister, Kamala (Jigri), and her husband Dr Pushkar Nath, already lived there. Over the years, many other cousins had arrived, a process that was hastened when the jihadists forced the expulsion of the Hindus from Kashmir in the 90s.

In Delhi she became the secretary of a group of women who wished to build a temple to Goddess Durgā. They went around for donations and finally a grand temple was constructed. The affairs of the temple were a responsibility that gave her satisfaction. She was astute in her judgment of people. She was also a fun-loving person who could clown around, which endeared her to the younger relatives.

After the passing of father, mother wanted to live independently in her apartment. She said she would manage all right for Shakti lived in the same neighborhood. During several visits to Delhi in the nineties, it was clear that despite putting on a brave face, father's loss had had a devastating effect on her.

After the six months she spent in Honolulu in 1994-1995, we could not persuade her to return to the United States. Eventually, we hit upon the idea of doing the thread ceremony for the boys and girls in the family in Maryland in December 1998 and convinced her that it couldn't be held without her. Subsequent to this she was in the United States every year for four to six months until 2007.

In the last five years of life she had to use oxygenating machines and nebulizers to help her breathe. But she remained the best host, ready to make tea or dinner for any guest who dropped in. Her mind was active, and she was abreast of politics of the day.

I talked to her regularly on phone, but my great regret is that I spent just a few days with her on each brief trip to India. I had urged her to keep writing in her diary, and when her earlier jottings were edited, it became the book of poems. The directness and simplicity of these poems carried much power. I was hoping that her more recent jottings would yield material that would go into her autobiography.

Fortuitously, I was in Delhi to give a lecture close to her 81st birthday, which marks the completion of 1,000 moons, and we had a small celebration.

22. Science and Consciousness

Investigating the mystery of consciousness has remained one of the constants of my professional career. I have approached it variously through logic, philosophy, neural networks and personal study.

The problem of consciousness went mainstream after the anesthesiologist Stuart Hameroff organized a series of conferences on it at the University of Arizona in Tucson, alternating with locations outside the US. This got neuroscientists, philosophers, computer scientists, physicists, scholars of religion and others to talk to each other on the subject.

The early motivation to study neural networks was the desire to build computing machines that worked like the brain. While the brain may not match the computer in numerical calculations, computers cannot match humans in judgment and insight.

I wrote many articles on neural networks in the 90s that got me connected to the famed brain scientist, psychologist and philosopher Karl Pribram and his wife, the novelist Katherine Neville. Pribram invited me to a workshop he had organized at Radford, Virginia, and asked me to contribute chapters to a book he was editing.

Pribram was born in 1919 in Vienna to a Czech father and Indonesian mother. He received his MD from the University of Chicago and for forty years he was professor first at Yale and then at Stanford. He did pioneering research into the functions of the limbic system, frontal lobes, temporal lobes and their roles in decision-making and emotion. He is credited with launching the cognitive revolution in psychology. He also proposed the holonomic theory of memory and perception that made him a star in the public imagination, and many popular books were written on this theory. He was a fine philosopher of the brain and he was the first laureate of the Dagmar and Vaclav Havel Award for uniting the sciences and the humanities.

We met many times at academic meetings and I invited him to speak at LSU in the Science and Religion Collegium. He was an extraordinary raconteur and I regret that I did not record anecdotes of his encounters with other science pioneers. His book *The Form Within,* which was published in 2013 one year before he died, presented an insider's view of brain research in the twentieth century. We were joint speakers at a meeting organized by the Gandhi Center in Washington in 2012, which was to be his last public meeting.

The idea of consciousness requires not only an awareness of things but also the awareness that one is aware. If awareness is some kind of a measurement, it should have a reference. This, in turn, poses two problems: first, what is the reference for awareness; and, second, how does consciousness choose between various possibilities?

The problem of the referent in awareness is an old one. The Vedic sages solved it by postulating a single universal, transcendental consciousness. In this view, the individual's empirical consciousness is a projection and the referent for it is the universal. The analogy of the same sun reflecting in a million different pots of water as little suns is provided to explain the empirical consciousness of the individual. The Māṇḍūkya Upaniṣad speaks of four basic states of consciousness: waking, dreaming, deep-sleep, and a fourth which transcends these three. The waking state is primarily concerned with the embodied self and sensations; in the dreaming self, not all memories associated with the autobiographical self are available to the conscious agent; in deep-sleep where there is no dreaming, the conscious self is dormant; and in the fourth state, the conscious self is in a transcendent state.

In a somewhat similar way, Plato invokes an object in a cave that cannot be seen directly and whose shadows on the wall represent the accessible phenomena. In this view, truth is an abstraction and universals exist independent of particulars.

In European philosophy, René Descartes proposed that consciousness resides within an immaterial domain of *res cogitans* (the realm of thought), to be contrasted from the domain of material things of *res extensa* (the realm of extension), and he assumed that the two realms interact in the brain, but the Cartesian dualist position is no longer taken seriously. Immanuel Kant arrived at a resolution similar to that of the Vedic tradition by arguing that empirical consciousness must have a necessary reference to a transcendental consciousness — a consciousness that precedes all particular experience. The universal or transcendental position is generally unacceptable to mainstream scientists who insist on reductionist models.

William James spoke of two kinds of selves: the self as knower (the "I"), and the self as known (the "me"). Each person's self is partly subjective (as knower) and partly objective (as known). The objective self itself may be described in its three aspects: the material self, the social self, and the spiritual self. Narrative self-reference is in contrast to the immediate, knowing "I" that supports the notion of momentary experience as an expression of selfhood.

James believed that as knower, the self is comprised of different mental states. Thought has no constant elements and every perception is relative and contextualized. States of mind are never repeated, and whereas objects might be constant and discrete, thought is constantly changing and mental states arise out of choices that are made by the mind. James believed that thought flows, and thus he could speak of a stream of consciousness.

If one were to find the boundaries between the "me" and the "I" of consciousness, it becomes essential to find a "minimal" sense of self. It is easy to speak of the intuition that there is a basic or primitive something that is the true self, and much harder to provide evidence for such belief. Conceptually, there must be something permanent — a bedrock — underlying the stream of consciousness. It is known that medial prefrontal cortex (mPFC) supports self-awareness by linking subjective experiences across time and it is of special importance for human social cognition and behavior. It plays a role in decision making, executive control, reward-guided learning, and recent and remote memories. Cortical midline processes support narrative self-reference that maintains continuity of identity across time. It has been proposed that the function of the mPFC is to learn associations between context, locations, events, and corresponding adaptive responses, particularly emotional ones. Therefore, neuropsychological accounts of episodic memory or loss of memory can help to define the neural bases of the narrative self.

The mechanisms associated with consciousness are often very dissimilar both spatially and temporally and may be associated with different perceptions. This is so, for example, for the specific cases of color and visual motion awareness. The disparate and multiple mechanisms of perception and comprehension lead to the view that consciousness has no single neural correlate. If lower-level consciousness states occur in different parts of the brain, the highest node in a hierarchical model of consciousness must be located in non-physical space and it could very well be a unitary state.

The quest for consciousness is also the final goal of artificial intelligence (AI). The claim that the universe itself is a giant machine complements the belief that true machine intelligence and self-awareness will arise after machine complexity has crossed a critical threshold.

But machines only follow instructions, and it is not credible that just the fact of a certain number of connections between computing units creates the property of self-awareness. But if machines will never become self-aware, why is the brain-machine conscious? The brain, unlike a computing machine, is a self-organizing system that responds to the nature and quality of its interaction with the environment. Since ecological systems are self-organizing, without being self-aware, one may conclude that while self-organization is a necessary pre-requisite for consciousness, it is not sufficient.

Cognitive scientists and biologists consider evolutionary aspects related to cognitive capacity, where consciousness is viewed as emerging out of language. Research on chimpanzees and bonobos reveals that although they can be taught basic vocabulary of several hundred words, this linguistic ability does not extend to syntax. According to the nativist view, language ability is rooted in the biology of the brain, and our ability to use grammar and syntax is an instinct, dependent on specific modules of the brain. We learn language as a consequence of a unique biological adaptation, and not because it is an emergent response to the problem of communication confronted by ourselves and our ancestors.

In my work, I have presented evidence that negates the view that the brain is an ordinary machine. I argue that even with self-organization and hitherto-unknown quantum characteristics some capacities of the mind will remain unexplainable. Individuals with anomalous abilities confirm that cognitive ability is not a simple processing of sensory information by a central intelligence extraction system.

––––––––

According to the reductionist view, brain and mind are identical and mind is the sum total of the activity in the brain, when viewed at a suitable higher level of representation. Opposed to this is the viewpoint that although mind requires a physical structure, it ends up transcending that structure.

The mind processes sensory inputs coming into the brain using its store of memories. A cognitive act is an active process where the selectivity of the sensory networks, and the accompanying processing in the brain, is organized based on the expectation of the cognitive task and on effort, will and intention. Intelligence is a result of the workings of numerous active cognitive agents.

The reductionist approach to artificial intelligence emerged out of an attempt to mechanize logic in the 1930s. In turn, AI and computer science influenced research in psychology and neuroscience and the view developed that a cognitive act is a logical computation. With the advent of quantum computing theory, we know that the mechanistic model of computing does not capture all the power of natural computation.

Schrödinger spoke of the arithmetic paradox related to the mind as being "the many conscious egos from whose mental experiences the one world is concocted." He added that there are only two ways out of the number paradox. "One way out is the multiplication of the world in Leibniz's fearful doctrine of monads: every monad to be a world by itself... [and the other is the Vedic] alternative, namely the unification of minds or consciousnesses."

Leibniz's monads are forms of being that are eternal, indecomposable, individual, subject to their own laws, un-interacting, with each reflecting the entire universe in pre-established harmony. This is too extravagant to be taken seriously.

The two hemispheres of the brain are linked by the rich connections of the corpus callosum. The visual system is arranged so that each eye normally projects to both hemispheres. By cutting the optic-nerve crossing, the chiasm, the remaining fibers in the optic nerve transmit information to the hemisphere on the same side. Visual input to the left eye is sent only to the left hemisphere, and input to the right eye projects only to the right hemisphere. The visual areas also communicate through the corpus callosum. When these fibers are also severed, the patient is left with a split brain.

Experiments have shown that cats with split brains did as well as normal cats when it came to learning the task of discriminating between a circle and a square in order to obtain a food reward, while wearing a patch on one eye. This showed that one half of the brain did as well at the task as both the halves in communication. When the patch was transferred to the other eye, the split-brain cats behaved different from the normal cats, indicating that their previous learning had not been completely transferred to the other half of the brain.

A human patient with left-hemisphere speech does not know what his right hemisphere has seen through the right eye. The information in the right brain is unavailable to the left brain and vice versa. The left brain responds to the stimulus reaching it whereas the right brain responds to its own input. Each half brain learns, remembers, and carries out planned activities. One may assume that the split-brain patient has lost conscious access to those cognitive functions that are regulated by the non-speech hemisphere. Or, one may say that nothing is changed as far as the awareness of the patient is considered and the cognitions of the right brain were linguistically isolated all along, even before the commissurotomy was performed. The procedure only disrupts the visual and other cognitive-processing pathways.

The patients themselves seem to support this second view. There seems to be no antagonism in the responses of the two hemispheres and the left hemisphere is able to fit the actions related to the information reaching the right hemisphere in a plausible theory. For example, consider the test where the word "pink" is flashed to the right hemisphere and the word "bottle" is flashed to the left. Several bottles of different colors and shapes are placed before the patient and he is asked to choose one. He immediately picks the pink bottle explaining that pink is a nice color. Although the patient is not consciously aware of the right eye having seen the word "pink" he, nevertheless, "feels" that pink is the right choice for the occasion. In this sense, this behavior is very similar to that of blindsight patients.

Patients with disrupted brains are quite certain that their awareness is whole. If shared activity was all there was to consciousness, this would have been destroyed or multiplied by commissurotomy. Split brains should then represent two minds just as in freak births with one trunk and two heads we do have two minds.

———

The Vedic texts claim to be ātmavidyā, "science of self" or "consciousness science." The cryptic Ṛgveda and the prose commentaries of the Brāhmaṇas and the Upaniṣads provide a framework to decode its narrative, establishing the central concern with consciousness.

In the Vedic view, reality is unitary at the deepest level since otherwise there would be chaos. This reality is called Brahman (neuter gender). Brahman engenders and, paradoxically, transcends the mind/matter split. It is identical to consciousness at the cosmic scale and it informs individual minds.

Since language is linear, whereas the unfolding of the universe takes place in a multitude of dimensions, language is limited in its ability to describe reality. Due to this limitation, reality can only be experienced and never described fully. All descriptions of the universe lead to logical paradox, and Brahman is the category transcending all oppositions.

I mentioned earlier that the Vedas classify knowledge in two ways: the higher or unified and the lower or dual. The higher knowledge concerns the perceiving subject (consciousness), whereas the lower knowledge concerns objects. The higher knowledge can be arrived at only through intuition and meditation on the paradoxes of the outer world. The lower knowledge is analytical and it represents standard science (śāstra) with its many branches. In addition, darśana represents philosophy where the problem of self is taken together with some aspect of outer reality. There is a complementarity between the higher and the lower, each being necessary to define the other. This complementarity mirrors the divide between mind and body.

23. Colors of Culture

I had never been to the Kumbha when I lived in India and so I was pleased when in early 2016 I received an invitation from Shivraj Singh Chouhan, the chief minister of Madhya Pradesh, to come and speak at the Mela. To ensure that I would not refuse the invite, Naumi was also invited. We flew to Delhi where we stopped for a few days to speak at the Sanskrit Department of Delhi University and to visit Naumi's alma mater Indraprastha College.

From Delhi we flew to Indore where our stay was in a superbly run hotel with arrangement to take us by car every day to the conference venue. The general level of development in the city with its wide avenues and glass-fronted buildings appeared impressive.

In the swirl of great social changes wrought by technology, one universal phenomenon that has escaped fundamental transformation is pilgrimage. Indeed, ease of transportation and modern accommodation has made the task of the pilgrim easier than ever before.

Tourism for pleasure has become big in recent years, but it is not quite pilgrimage, because that involves hardship necessary for the person to introspect and reflect on one's life.

While religious journeying remains popular on all continents, India is the granddaddy of pilgrimage with the seekers going to mountains and ancient temples, to crossing points (tirthas) on the rivers, and to Kumbha Melas, where tens of millions of people assemble to take a ritual bath.

Traditionally, the Kumbha served as the meeting place of the sadhus of different sects. Planning for the Kumbha at Ujjain, Shivraj Singh Chouhan proposed that intellectuals, civic leaders, writers, and thinkers should similarly come together to confer on problems confronting not only Indias, but outsiders as well. Since this was the first time such a meeting was to be held it was given the name Vichar Mahakumbha.

This is a brilliant idea that enlarges the scope of the Kumbha and I hope it will be repeated at other Melas. The 2016 Vichar Mahakumbha, which was organized in Ninora Village not far from Ujjain, was a tremendous success with speakers and participants from several countries. The talks were on five major themes: (i) Living the right way; (ii) Cleanliness and ecology; (iii) Agriculture and crafts; (iv) Sustainable development and climate change; and (v) Empowerment of vomen. I was asked to speak on the issues facing sustainable development and I highlighted the challenge of jobs in our age of machines.

According to tradition, the origin of the Kumbha is in the primeval *samudra manthana* (churning of the ocean) by the asuras and the devas. The purpose of this churning is amrita (nectar of immortality) that both the devas and the asuras covet. At last, as the churning proceeds, the kumbha appears and in the struggle between the two parties to get hold of it, amrita spills at four places: Haridwar, Prayag, Nashik, and Ujjain on the banks of Ganga, the confluence of Ganga and Yamuna, Godavari, and Kshipra, respectively.

The samudra manthana is one of the central themes of the Vedas, and it takes place not only at the cosmic level but also in the heart of each individual as captured by the dictum *yat brahmāṇḍe tad piṇḍe (*as in the cosmos, so in the cell). The seeker wishes to connect to the cosmos by journeying to the Mela where the amrita fell. In this he is guided by Brihaspati (Jupiter), the teacher of the devas and the pilgrimage is completed with a bath in the river.

The orbit of Jupiter is twelve years, and so the Kumbha comes around with this frequency. The specific month is determined by the conjunction of Jupiter with the nakṣatra associated with the place. The Ujjain Kumbha Mela takes place when Jupiter enters Leo (Simha) which explains its other name, the Simhastha. Every 144 years, the Mela is a Mahakumbha.

The Chinese traveler Xuanzang described a mass bathing ritual held in the reign of Emperor Harsha in 644 CE at the confluence of Ganga and Yamuna at Prayaga. It is believed that the festival at Ujjain was classed as Kumbha in the 18th century, with Ranoji Rao Shinde, a general to Peshwa Bajirao, inviting sadhus from Nashik to organize it.

When he visited the Kumbha Mela of Allahabad (now called Prayagraj) in 1895, Mark Twain was told that two million pilgrims came to the Mela. He spoke of his experience thus: "It is wonderful, the power of a faith like that, that can make multitudes upon multitudes of the old and weak and the young and frail enter without hesitation or complaint upon such incredible journeys and endure the resultant miseries without repining. It is done in love, or it is done in fear; I do not know which it is. No matter what the impulse is, the act born of it is beyond imagination marvelous to our kind of people, the cold whites."

The Kumbha Melas were traditionally managed by the akhārās, but now the general arrangements are made by the government. The Melas are the greatest peaceful congregations of people on earth and there are reports that the Prayagraj Kumbha of 2013 attracted nearly 120 million people.

Pushkaram (or just Pushkar) is another festival dedicated to the worshiping of twelve sacred rivers that range from Ganga to Kaveri. This celebration is at specific temples along the banks in a manner quite like the Kumbha. Each river is associated with a zodiac sign, and the river for each year's festival is based on the conjunction of the river sign with Jupiter. The Pushkaram in September 2017 will be on the banks of the Kaveri River.

To find the balance in one's own life there is nothing as instructive as getting lost and rendered anonymous in the vast multitudes of the Kumbha. This is one of the reasons the Westerner is so fascinated by these congregations. The Melas, the Pushkarams and other pilgrimages are a wonderful system of spiritual journey across the entire land of India. They offer participation in a deeply personal yet universal act that has the potential to heal and let each person connect with the larger current of humanity.

After the Kumbha, we spent some days in Dehra Dun. From there we visited Landour for it is one of the very few Raj-era towns in India that has changed little in the past seventy years. Apart from its old churches and stone paved pathways, it offers the most amazing sight of the Himalayas. It is next to Mussoorie but somehow on my previous visits I had never taken the road to it.

We took the narrow road beyond Mussoorie that goes up Lal Tibba to Landour Bazaar and Char Dukan, which has several nice eating-places, with St. Paul's Church rising on the side. Car traffic beyond Char Dukan is not allowed without special permission, so we took the stone-paved road past the Church to the far end of the town.

Many of the buildings in Landour are part of the Cantonment and it is estimated that there are just 100 detached houses and cottages. We walked past many of these buildings till we reached the Kellogg Church and the Kellogg

Language School and beyond it discovered The Corner Shop, which is a delightful coffee shop.

The traveler Emily Eden, who was in Landour in 1838, was charmed by the sight of the Himalayas, declaring: "it is impossible to imagine more beautiful scenery." She was speaking of the magnificent view of the Char Dham of Yamunotri, Gangotri, Kedarnath, and Badrinath flanked by Svargarohini on the west and Nanda Devi on the east. Svargarohini is the mountain that, according to the Mahābhārata, the Pandavas in their old age decided to climb to reach the heavens, with only Yudhishthira and his dog succeeding, and Nanda Devi is the famous peak named after the goddess who brings happiness.

Up the Country: Letters from India is Emily Eden's account of travels through north India from 1837 to 1840. Emily was the sister of George Eden, Lord Auckland, who was the Governor General of India from 1836 to 1842, and she was to spend two and a half years with him. The book is an important chronicle of the East India Company Rule in early nineteenth century, providing a graphic account of travels through heat and dust of the plains, vignettes of the courts at Delhi and Lahore, and sojourn in Shimla which served as the summer capital of India.

Emily Eden was a well-known society lady in 19th century England, who was a close friend of William Lamb, Viscount Melbourne, Queen Victoria's first prime minister, after whom Melbourne, Australia, is named (whereas Auckland is named after Emily's brother). Their mutual friends had hoped that the two would marry, because Viscount Melbourne was widowed when not yet fifty and Emily was a most eligible lady, but somehow it did not happen.

Perhaps Melbourne's unhappy years with his deceased wife, Caroline Lamb, had made him fearful of another marriage. Caroline had had a passionate and scandalous affair with Lord Byron, the poet. After Byron broke off the relationship under pressure from Melbourne's mother, Caroline stalked him until he publicly insulted her and she slashed her wrists, which Byron called a theatrical performance. After his wife's death, Melbourne made himself disagreeable to potential suitors like Emily Eden by profanity and odd behavior. Rather than keep on waiting for him to propose and knowing that his prime ministership made it unlikely that he would find time to do so, Emily decided to leave the glittering social circuit of London to follow her brother to India.

In Emily Eden's time, the paths in Mussoorie and Landour were narrow and she did some sightseeing atop a jonpaun, sedan-chair with bearers in orange and brown livery, but when she saw jonpauns pass each other at the bends at high speed, she was scared that somebody was going to go down the edge. On one occasion, she had to get down her pony and lead it across one of the narrowest sections of the path.

On our way back to Char Dukan from the Corner Store via the north ridge, we saw the scene of the Himalayas that Emily Eden had raved about. The Char Dham were shining in the snowy reaches of the Himalayas across the horizon.

Next day, Naumi, her brother Shiven and I left Dehra Dun on a trip to Chakrata. Our driver, a cheerful Jaunsāri, had many stories to tell us about his family and the region. After a drinks break at a mango orchard in Herbertpur, we stopped at Kalsi which is about 45 kilometers northwest of Dehra Dun.

Kalsi is famous for the only Aśokan Edict in north India, and it also has remains of an altar constructed for a royal Aśvamedha rite performed in the third century.

Situated at the confluence of Yamuna and Tons rivers, beyond it to the west is Himachal Pradesh. Tons is the larger river at the join, and many have theorized that it is the Vedic Sarasvati which, in ancient times, flowed parallel to the Yamuna, meeting it much further down in Haryana.

The edict is inscribed on quartz rock which is 10 feet high, 10 feet wide, and 8 feet deep at its base. Like most other edicts, it is in Prakrit written in Brahmi script, and it appears to have been issued somewhat before 250 BCE. It describes Aśoka's policies, reforms and injunctions for good citizenship. The prescriptions include self-control, purity of mind, gratitude, service to parents and ascetics, alms to brahmins and śramaṇas, proper behavior towards friends, relatives, and servants, and concordance in religious matters. The edict also speaks of the lands in the south and the west where Aśoka sent his embassies to spread the message of dharma.

After seeing the edict and a stroll in the bazaar, we drove another fifty kilometers north through mountain road to Chakrata, which is at 7000 feet (2,200 meters). The climb begins just beyond Kalsi and crossing a couple of ranges, much climbing and many twists and turns, Chakrata appears to float from afar as a shining city on the top of the mountain range. But it takes further hilly driving before one arrives.

The area is inhabited by the Jaunsār and the Bāwar people, who claim descent from the Pāṇḍavas and the Kauravas, respectively, and speak Pahari. As in many other Himalayan regions, polyandry is a common custom to keep the population in check. This practice, in which brothers marry one wife (like Draupadī of the Mahābhārata), is something I knew of in Ladakh during my boyhood years. In Ladakh, the unmarried girls were packed off to the monastery to train as nuns; in Jaunsār-Bāwar, the polyandry

195

of the poorer people is somewhat balanced by the polygamy of the richer folk.

Chakrata was established as a cantonment by the British in 1869. With soldiers came the need for alcohol, and the Imperial Gazetteer of 1909 speaks of a brewery with 30 employees and production of 88,000 gallons. Then, its population was 1,200; now it is three times as much.

Chakrata is a hill station for the quiet traveler with many trails for the trekker. The bazaar, which mercifully is only for pedestrians, reminded me of the bazaars of small towns in the Jammu and Kashmir of my childhood. As a regiment town, the shops are well stocked with all kinds of things for the soldier and his family.

From what we saw, SUVs appear to be the main transport of the locals. Many of these were frightfully overloaded with some passengers sitting on the roof. Accidents do happen from time to time with much loss of life.

The visit to Kalsi reminds one of the 12-yearly Nanda Devi Raj Jat (Jat is short for Skt. Yatra) that recreates the return of the local princess Nanda, who is now Śiva's wife, to the mountainous abode of her husband. Nanda is carried in a litter together with other gifts and offerings. The 12-year period appears to be from the cycle for Brihaspati as in the Kumbha.

The foundational basis of the festival is astronomical for Śiva is the Sun. But Śiva is also universal consciousness and, therefore, the originators of this festival thought of a way to connect it to one of the most moving ceremonies in village life that makes one confront eternal questions of love, compassion, and meaning.

In traditional India, the hardest hearts melted and relatives wept when the family bid goodbye to the newlywed daughter before she set out to go with her husband to some far village. Remember, the daughter was very young, and she had seen her husband for the first time at the just-concluded wedding ceremony, and she knew no one at her new village. For part of the journey the natal family walked with her until the final goodbyes were spoken.

She did return to her natal home from time to time and at the end of the visit that could last a few days or longer, she was sent off ceremoniously just as after the wedding, although with each successive visit the pain of the parting got lesser. In these subsequent sendoffs also she was given new gifts and things she would need at her home.

The Uttarakhandis believe that the goddess Nanda is their princess. Nanda is another name for Parvati, the daughter of the King of the Himalayas, who resolved to marry Śiva, the Yogi, although he lived alone on the Kailash Mountain. In order to attract the notice of Śiva, she performs yogic austerities and lives without food which earns her the nickname Aparna, one who doesn't even eat the leaves of trees. Śiva hears of her and comes in disguise to dissuade her, telling her of how difficult her life would be as Śiva's wife. Nanda remains unmoved and finally Śiva accepts her and they get married. The residents of the Mountain Kingdom are happy that she will be the wife to the Great God but they are also sad that she is going to be very lonely at Śiva's place where most of the time he is absorbed in his meditation.

Every twelve years, Nanda is back with her people and now is the time for her to return to Kailash. The procession starts from a village near Karnaprayag with a four-horned sheep in the front. Thousands take part in the procession singing and dancing and carrying the dola (litter) of Nanda. The processionists walk nearly 150 miles in three weeks through mountain villages and fastnesses to the 16,500 ft. Roopkund (a glacial lake) where goodbyes to the beloved princess Nanda are made and the four-horned sheep is set free and imagined to accompany the princess to the higher mountains beyond.

Some believe that the Nanda Devi processions and fairs started in Kumaon during the reign of the King Kalyan Chand in the 16th century; others think that the tradition is much older and it goes back to the 9th century. A smaller annual Nanda Jat is also celebrated.

––––––––––

We visited two very different countries in the following weeks. First, we were in south Sweden in Växjö where I was presenting a paper on the epistemology of communication at a quantum theory conference. This paper was different from most others in arguing for the mind that must be presumed if we speak of information in physics. We also visited Copenhagen and Stockholm and then took a train to Oslo.

The markets in all these towns had many women wearing hijab and veil, reflecting the large number of recent migrants from the Islamic world. We also saw beggars, quite like what we had seen in France the previous year. One consequence of joining the European Union is the loss of sovereignty in the policing of borders.

Welfare benefits are the magnet that is driving people from poorer nations to migrate and since they come from cultures that are very different to that of Europe they will not assimilate. The general atmosphere is of wariness. For protection against terrorism, the entrance to the police station at Copenhagen train station is through an automated screening room where the visitor is checked for weapons and bombs. We discovered this when we went to the station to make a call to the US about a lost credit card.

Some call Stockholm the Venice of the North for its many waterways; it also has a charming old town called

Gamlastan, and the great Vasa Museum with the reconstructed ship that sank 20 minutes after it was launched in 1628. Copenhagen has its mermaid and the commune of Christiania, where people with bandana-covered faces sell drugs openly.

To my mind the Nordic capital with the most old-worldly allure is Oslo. Right through the middle of the city is River Akerselva with tea and coffee shops here and there that takes one into pre-industrial 19th century recalling the descriptions of Ibsen, Hugo, Hardy, and the incomparable Russian masters. The waterfalls of Akerselva were used for power by the industry of the mid-nineteenth century. Oslo has a charming waterfront from where one can take boats to nearby islands or the promenade to the royal palace up the hill.

Oslo'sFram Museum houses the ships associated with the great polar explorers Fridtjof Nansen, Otto Sverdrup and Roald Amundsen. Its other attractive sights include the Vigeland Sculpture Park with nudes in all kinds of situations, and the Munch Museum. One wonders how long the public display of the human form will be allowed to stand since Europe now has angry people who want no such representation.

———

Next we traveled to Perth for another visit to Curtin University. Beautiful like other Australian cities, a section of its business district is a pedestrian-only mall with alleys on the side with quaint little shops and cafes. The city is served by a system of five different bus routes that are free to everyone. It has many parks including the huge King's Park on the hill at one side. The Swan River, which looks like a swan with narrow curved neck and broad body, flows through the city and black swans may be seen swimming in its waters. On one side is the wonderful Kings Park on the hill with its magnificent 750-year old boab tree that I make a point to visit on each trip to the city. The residents of Perth like to remind visitors that they live in the most isolated city in the world for it is closer to Bali in Indonesia than any of the large Australian cities.

After two weeks in Perth, during which time we explored the city and its environs well, we decided to take a day trip. Opening our tourist guide map, Naumi and I saw a rather big circle north of Perth, a place called Cervantes, and we decided to go there. Knowing of Miguel de Cervantes, whose novel *Don Quixote* I had read with great enjoyment as a child, I was glad to have this opportunity to visit a city named after him.

I must begin by saying that I didn't quite enjoy driving in Australia. That the driving is on the left of the road, rather than the right of the United States, was a problem for a week or so, and I had made the mistake of not renting a car with GPS and lost my way on more than one occasion. More seriously, traffic lanes in Australia are much narrower compared to those in the United States and from time to time the road switches between 4-lanes to 2-lanes and I hate drivers pushing me from behind. Fortunately, my rental car was a small Ford and, therefore, the narrowness of the lanes was not as big a cognitive problem as I had feared.

We first drove along the Indian Ocean Drive and in about an hour were at Yanchep National Park, which is famous for koalas and kangaroos. It so turned out that the few koalas we saw were mostly sleepy and the kangaroos were quite scrawny. But the scenery was superb and we took couple of trails to explore the flora of the park. Naumi bought some keepsakes at the park shop.

Next we drove two hours along sandhills with wonderful vistas of the Indian Ocean stopping a couple of times to appreciate spring blooms (it was late July). As we exited the ramp leading to the destination, a big billboard announced, "Welcome to Cervantes, Population 732." The size of the circle next on the map should not have misled us for the entire population of Western Australia (which is about 40 percent of the continent) is only 2.6 million, of which 2.1 million are residents of Perth, but I had not paid attention to this fact.

It was past lunch at the famous lobster shack of Cervantes, but we found a small café that served superb tea and biscuits. Behind the café was the beach and we got to walk up and down on it although we were the only souls there. The charming lady at the café shop told us that the name of the village was only indirectly after the great Spanish writer; it was named after a ship that was wrecked here and not all know of the origin of the ship's name.

The Pinnacles Desert, which is part of the Nambung National Park, is less than half-hour drive from Cervantes. The Park was full of visitors and after visiting the Pinnacles Desert Discovery Centre where we learnt new facts about the geology of the region, we followed other visitors on tracks and trails leading through thousands of limestone spires formed over millions of years. I was surprised when told that the limestone of the Pinnacles came from seashells from an earlier era rich in marine life. The spires are of different shapes and sizes and the landscape looks out of this world. On our way back, we skirted Lake Thetis, which is well known for its stromatolites, watched the sun set into the Indian Ocean, and returned to Perth without incident.

In the drive up and down the coast from Perth, the serpentine Darling Scarp sits to the east. The Noongar people, who lived here before the Europeans but are less than 4% of the population of Western Australia now, saw the Scarp as a dreamtime creature, a rainbow serpent called

201

Wagyl, who was responsible for the emergence of the Swan and the Canning Rivers. They saw the Wagyl shape the land by its tracks, scouring out the course of the rivers and creating bays and lakes when it rested. Piles of rocks were its droppings, and its scales became the forests and woodlands of the region.

Some call the dreamtime "time out of time" or "everywhen" when one is joined to primeval mind. It is the arch of existence that liberates one from one's ordinary conditioned reality. Not to be taken literally as some academics do, it connects the topography of the land to the topography of the mind. The traveling trails of dreaming are songlines that cut across the continent, quite like how the Ganga and the Sarasvati have parallels in the physiological structures of the brain and songs of the poets.

Sadly, the dreamtime offers no protection from the present and the last two centuries have been a period of unspeakable suffering for the Noongar. The ones amongst them who cried out were banished to the penal settlement of the inhospitable Rottnest Island, just off Perth, and, until sixty years ago, they were subject to the Native Welfare Act, in which one-third of the people were placed in state-run concentration camps and nearly a quarter of the children forcibly adopted. These stolen children like other aboriginal children were removed from their families by the Australian government agencies and church missions under acts of parliament. In December 2007, the Australian prime minister issued an apology to the indigenous Australians for this mistreatment.

Mt. Eliza, known in Noongar language as *Kaarta gar-up* and *Mooro Katta,* which is now a part of Kings Park that overlooks Perth, is a sacred mountain to the Noongars. The swan-like shape of the water below it must have generated mystery and awe. Strong buildings or skyscrapers are not sacred places because they represent the power of man. Perth pays homage to this latter power not only with its marvelous buildings but also with its theater, opera, and performing arts.

———————

About fifty years ago, a few pioneers from Perth set up vineyards in the Margaret River area, and these wines have attained international fame. Named after the eponymous river, the area is also famous for its beaches, caves and surfing spots. It was a cold July day so we were not thinking of the sea and the beach; it looked like a good day to visit a cave and sample a few wineries.

The town, which is two-and-a-half hour from Perth, is just a few streets and its economy is organized around the traveler. The road to it runs along picturesque tree-lined avenues along the highway. The forests around this and other caves have karri and marri trees that are common in southwest Australia.

Three weirs have been constructed on the Margaret River within the town. They come with fish ladders to enable the upstream migration of native fish and lamprey. The river and its tributaries have many permanent pools that are a summer refuge for various river animals including water birds, turtles, water rats, fish and crayfish.

The land between the town of Margaret River and Indian Ocean is of limestone rocks. The caves of the region are a result of the dissolution of limestone by acidic water caused by erosion over thousands to millions of years. These caves have their own underground drainage systems that contribute to the erosion. One of the biggest of these is the Mammoth Cave that has fossils of fauna over 35,000 years old, including those of marsupial dog and the giant marsupial herbivore Zygomaturus, which was like a pouched pygmy hippopotamus.

It is straightforward to reach Mammoth Cave although its entrance through the trees, with whistling birds and attractive flowering plants, is easy to miss. The cave chambers are huge with boardwalks and platforms, which help the visitor see the details. A seasonal stream meanders through the cave. At many places the stalagmites rise from the floor as pillars of decreasing size that do not quite make it to the ceiling and clumps of stalactites descend from the ceiling, and there are places where they meet to form pillars. This was one of the underground haunts of the rainbow serpent.

Who can believe that someone would think of a small-scale replication of Venice with its waterways and bridges in faraway Australia? Perhaps it shouldn't surprise us. Remember how the London Bridge ended up in Arizona? In 1963, two wealthy promoters of a new city out in the desert thought of the publicity they will receive if they purchased the ancient London Bridge, which was going to be demolished in 1968. They paid a couple of million dollars for it, although it took a few millions more to disassemble the bridge, mark the stones, and assemble them back, but it put them on the map and now Lake Havasu City is a flourishing place with over 52,000 residents.

Even more striking than erecting a monument at a faraway place is copycat architecture. It is seen all over the world but nowhere has it been done as assiduously as in China. Bianca Bosker has written a fascinating book titled *Original Copies* where she describes the Chinese tradition of architectural mimicry. A one-third-scale Eiffel

Tower rises above Champs Elysées Square in Hangzhou. Chengdu has a residential complex in the image of Dorchester, England. Shanghai's Thames Town has mock Tudor frontages, cobbles, squares, and corner shops. Around Shanghai are other suburbs that replicate Dutch, Italian, Canadian and Scandinavian-style developments.

The Venice on the Indian Ocean mimics the real Venice only in its general idea of houses on canals. It is at Mandurah, 72 kilometers south of Perth, which is Western Australia's second largest city even though its population is less than 100,000. It came strongly recommended for a weekend visit. We were pressed for time and so we decided to make it a daylong trip. We boarded the Transperth train to Mandurah at the Elizabeth Quay train station at the Swan River.

The indigenous people called this area Mandjoogoodap, "meeting place of the heart." The British simplified this name to Mandurah. Thomas Peel brought European settlement to the area in 1830 when he was granted 250,000 acres of land. We are told that Mandurah is the least affordable city in Australia.

A bus from the train station took us to the visitor center at the lake-like Peel Inlet where we purchased tickets for the cruise through the canals of Mandurah. The cruise boat left the dock near Cicarello's Restaurant, famed for its seafood, and rounded Stingray Point to the entrance to the Marina and docked at Dolphin Quay so that we could walk over the Ocean Marina Bridge. As we headed back out to the channel, we passed the little Venice area that comprises of canals surrounded by apartment buildings.

Back in the channel, we saw dolphins frolicking in the waters. Now the boat entered a complex of man-made canals with expensive homes. Many had their own private boats docked at their personal jetties. We were told that the houses are beautifully illuminated during the Christmas holidays.

Leaving the area comprised of homes, we went past Sutton Farm with its still standing limestone buildings. Eleanor and John Sutton, who arrived on the *Hindoo* in 1839, established Sutton Farms and became prominent settlers in the Mandurah area in the first decades of the colony. The farm operated as a dairy for the town and was one of the few regular places of employment in the late 1800s until the introduction of bottled milk around this time led to the dairy's decline. In 1924, Joseph Cooper bought the farm although it continued to be managed by the Sutton family. In 1989, Cedar Woods took ownership of the site and it became part of the Port Mandurah development.

After our cruise was over, we walked over the footbridge and by the many shops and restaurants along the way in the Dolphin Quay area. Then we made our way past the marina, through a housing development to the breakwater facing the ocean.

Perth offers lessons for regulated development that other cities can use. But Australia's isolation has protected it from uncontrolled migration.

———

One of the pleasures of travel is the encounter with the familiar at the most unlikely places. It forces attention on forms and designs that were glossed over as part of one's childhood world. The unfamiliar awakens the powers of observation. One gets to know more of the cultural spaces of the faraway regions than one's own.

Even though the pagoda form of the temple arose in India, one pays little attention to it in its native setting. An old theory sees the word *pagoda* derived from the name of a gold coin that was current in India in the 18th century. On one side of the coin was the form of the Goddess, *Bhagavati*, and on the other the shape of a terraced temple. The Austrian missionary and Sanskritist Paulinus of St. Bartholomew (1748-1806), who lived in Southern India during 1774-1789, informs that the coin was called Bhagavati. Specifically, it was a Durgi, for it had the image of Durgā.

The name of the coin in rapid colloquial speech sounded like *pagode* or *pagoda* to the Europeans but they wrongly associated it with the shape of the temple. In time, other gold coins issued by various Indian kings were also called pagoda by the Europeans, although their local names were determined by the imprint like Rāma, Varāha, Matsya, Venkateśvara, and so on and their value varied based on the purity of gold. Col Thomas Munro writing in 1806 about the Bellary district observed that there were 32 kinds of pagodas and 16 kinds of rupees (silver coins).

Paulinus, the first European to notice that Sanskrit and European languages belonged to the same family and publish a grammar of Sanskrit in Europe, lived in India around the time that the term pagoda came into European usage. James Prinsep (1799-1840) is responsible for popularizing the erroneous view that the term pagoda is derived from the shape of the pyramidal temple depicted on one side of the coin. The common Tamil name for the gold coin was Varāha from the imprint of the boar on the obverse side of the most popular coin.

My wife and I would have missed the much-loved Brisbane Pagoda but for our friends and long-term residents Prabhakar Murthy and his wife Jayashree, who declared it a sight not to be missed. They explained that it served as the Nepal Pavilion for World Expo '88 and it became so popular that the city decided to install it at the northwestern end of the South Bank Parklands on the bank of the Brisbane River.

We were staying at a hotel on the Spring Hill that sits above the Central Business District of the city. From there, we first walked by the Roma Street Parklands with its Mahatma Gandhi statue. Next came the Old Windmill, the oldest surviving building in Queensland, which was built by convicts in the colonial era to grind grains. The Windmill originally had wind-powered sails and also a treadwheel. From there the pedestrian-only zone of the city are nearby as is the bridge on the river.

The pagoda form, with its tiered roofs, is believed to have evolved from the *stupa*. I particularly like wooden pagodas with their multiple eaves and simplicity of conception. The ancient Pashupatinath Temple on the Bagmati River in Kathmandu is an early example of the wooden pagoda. According to historians, the pagoda form was taken from Nepal to China in the seventh century from where it spread to the other eastern countries. The Malla kings built some of the greatest pagodas in Nepal.

The pagoda is now associated more with China than India. It is amusing that another common word associated with China, *mandarin*, comes from the Sanskrit for minister or official, *mantrin*. The Indian interlocutors told the Portuguese that the Chinese officials they wished to meet were *mantrin* and the word stuck and eventually became the name of the influential variety of the Chinese language that the officials spoke.

As a student of temple architecture, it has long been my wish to visit the great wooden temples of Nepal in Kathmandu, Patan, and Bhaktapur, for these and other similar temples in the mountains of India constitute a unique branch of Indian temple architecture. But somehow it has not come to pass. So I was mighty pleased when I realized that Brisbane's Pagoda is a replica of the Pashupatinath Temple.

Craftsmen from 160 families worked on the Brisbane Pagoda in Kathmandu over a two-year period. The pieces were fashioned out of Terai timber, shipped to Australia, and assembled at the Expo site on the Brisbane River by Australian workers under Nepalese supervision.

The pagoda has images representing the different incarnations of Śiva and the Buddha, and an image of Avalokiteśvara, the deity of compassion. The Peace Pagoda is used for weddings and other private functions, and it also has benches for personal meditation. The pagoda is just a ferry-ride away from the University of Queensland campus.

24. Tesla, Vivekananda and the Akashic Field

I had for years been vaguely aware that Nikola Tesla and Swami Vivekananda had met, so when I heard from Deepak Chopra that he wished for me to speak at his Sages and Scientists Symposium in September 2016, I thought I should investigate this further.

Tesla is not well known these days in spite of the eponymous electric car, a technological tour de force that is expected to take automotive industry in a new direction. But 120 years ago he was a superstar. He competed with Thomas Edison over what should be the industry standard for power transmission. Tesla was for AC and Edison for DC, and as we know Tesla won and so in the sense of the delivery of electric power, we live in the Age of Tesla.

Born in 1856, Tesla studied engineering in Graz, Austria, but never graduated. He immigrated to the United States in 1884, and very soon had financial backing for laboratories and companies to develop a range of electrical devices. He was a pioneer of AC electricity, induction motor, X-rays, and he contributed to the development of radio and television. He invented the Tesla coil to generate high voltage, low current and high frequency alternating-current electricity with possible use in wireless power transmission. As futurist, he speculated on various technological possibilities for man, visualizing robots that he called teleautomatons, flying machines that used ambient energy and systems that exploited solar power.

After his death in 1943, he fell into relative obscurity. But in 1960 the General Conference on Weights and Measures named the SI unit of magnetic flux density the tesla in his honor, and thus science has immortalized his name.

It is generally accepted that Vivekananda changed the world by bringing the movement of self-knowledge to America and influencing some of the greatest minds of the twentieth century. He is also a giant of modern India who, through his life and inspired writing, contributed to the re-awakening of a nation. As the prime disciple of Sri Ramakrishna, he has been a part of my consciousness ever since I was a boy.

His international fame began with his address on 11 September 1893 at The Parliament of the World's Religions at the Art Institute of Chicago as part of the World's Columbian Exposition. He began his speech on behalf of "the most ancient order of monks in the world, the Vedic order of sannyasins, a religion which has taught the world both tolerance, and universal acceptance." Vivekananda quoted two illustrative passages from the Śiva-mahimā-strotam: "As the different streams having their sources in different places all mingle their water in the sea, so, O Lord, the different paths which men take, through different tendencies, various though they appear, crooked or straight, all lead to Thee!" and "Whosoever comes to Me, through whatsoever form, I reach him; all men are struggling through paths that in the end lead to Me."

In his visits to the West, Vivekananda met with the leading intellectuals and scientists. His followers and admirers in the West included the psychologist William James, the physicist Lord Kelvin, Nikola Tesla, the French actress Sarah Bernhardt, and the novelist Leo Tolstoy. He also influenced writers such as Romain Rolland, Aldous Huxley, Christopher Isherwood, and J.D. Salinger.

The actress Sarah Bernhardt, who was touring the United States, introduced Tesla and Vivekananda at a party she had given. This is what Vivekananda had to say of that meeting in a letter dated February 13, 1896: "Mr. Tesla was charmed to hear about the Vedantic prāṇa and ākāśa and the kalpas. He thinks he can demonstrate mathematically that force and matter are reducible to potential energy. I am to go to see him next week to get this mathematical demonstration. In that case Vedantic cosmology will be placed on the surest of foundations. I clearly see their perfect union with modern science, and the elucidation of one will be followed by that of the other."

We have no evidence that Tesla and Vivekananda met again. The equivalence of mass and energy in terms of the equation $E=mc^2$ was published just a few years afterwards by the Italian geologist Olinto de Pretto in 1903 and Albert Einstein in 1905.

In any event, Tesla, in his search of the ākāśic field, was looking for something more than converting matter into energy. His objective was to harness the primal energy within space itself for mankind's benefit.

In a posthumously published article called Man's Greatest Achievement, which was written in 1907, Tesla wrote about the use of ākāśa and prāṇa to solve mankind's greatest problems:

"Long ago [mankind] recognized that all perceptible matter comes from a primary substance, or tenuity beyond conception, filling all space, the Akasha or luminiferous ether, which is acted upon by the life giving Prana or creative force, calling into existence, in never ending cycles all things and phenomena. The primary substance, thrown into infinitesimal whirls of prodigious velocity, becomes gross matter; the force subsiding, the motion ceases and matter disappears, reverting to the primary substance."

How are we to interpret prāṇa and ākāśa of Vivekananda and Tesla? The prāṇa in Vedanta is the vital force of life, and the ākāśa is the element often translated as ether from which other elements emerge.

Prāṇa is more than breath; it is the subtle energy that guides the processes of the body. Modern medical science may not accept it, but the sadhus living in the upper reaches of the Himalayas in winter, or a modern man like Wim Hof in climbing 22,000 feet of Mount Everest in nothing but shorts and shoes speak of the mastery over it.

The Chāndogya Upaniṣad says this of the relationship between the elements of the universe: From the self (ātman) ākāśa arose; from ākāśa air; from air fire; from fire water; from water the earth. In the Śānti Parva in the Mahābhārata, the sequence of dissolution of the physical universe is as follows: Under extreme heat, earth becomes water, then fire, then wind, then ākāśa, then space, then mind, then time, then energy, and finally universal consciousness.

The fact that energy can be generated from primordial ether (ākāśa) is a fundamental tenet in the Vedas. The element ākāśa also generates other material elements. Therefore, much before the mass to energy transformation became established physics, Vivekananda was speaking of it and also of how the mind through prāṇa can do things that are outside the pale of known medical science.

More recently, it has become accepted that the vacuum state is associated with zero-point energy with measurable effects. Indeed the vacuum is teeming with creation and destruction of particles.

The idea of the ākāśic field as the medium of consciousness has caught some peoples' attention. Amongst these is the Hungarian scientist Ervin László who posits a field of information as the substance of the cosmos. But if it is information, it must come with a mind.

Although Vedanta and Vaiśeṣika postulate that the ākāśa is a field, it cannot be the field that carries consciousness. Consciousness is not an entity like other fields of physics because if it were so then the equations of physics are incomplete.

Both Vivekananda and Tesla were hoping for a mutual confirmation of Vedanta and physics. But time was not ripe and physics was to bring in observers (albeit indirectly) only thirty years later through the framework of quantum mechanics.

Now with the understanding of the zero-point energy of the vacuum and of the cognitive system through the discipline of neuroscience, we may be much closer to explaining the interplay of prāṇa and ākāśa.

There were several presentations made at the Sages Symposium that brought up to date new developments of physics, biology and medicine.

According to standard cosmology, the visible universe has less than one percent of the total energy of the universe, with dark matter and dark energy accounting for nearly 96% and interstellar dust nearly another 4%. According to another theory, dark matter is spread, filament like, across the universe, somewhat like the neural pathways of the brain.

I have long been familiar with the finding that the brain is plastic and our thoughts and actions lead to its reorganization. The more recent field of epigenetics shows learnt behavior can be passed on to the next generation via the epigenome. In a famous experiment in this field, laboratory rats were given electric shock subsequent to release of cherry odor. Soon they associated the odor with the shock and they cowered in the corners of the cage as soon as the odor was released.

The offspring of these rats were also fearful of the cherry odor even though they had never been given electric shock. It is believed that mental states affect chemicals that surround DNA causing it to change its three-dimensional structure that influences the expression of genes. Thus epigenetic inheritance is the transmittance of information from one generation of an organism to the next that affects the traits of offspring without alteration of the primary structure of DNA.

Yet another important development in biology is the microbiome which is the genetic information in the trillions of microbes in the body and this information is about hundred times more than the information in the organism's DNA although the microorganisms account for only 1-3% of the total body mass. Some have suggested that microorganisms govern the mammalian immune system, and the microbiome may play a role in autoimmune diseases like diabetes, muscular dystrophy, multiple sclerosis, and even some cancers.

25. The Sutra Trilogy

In the winter of 2015 I received an invitation from an editor to write a longish encyclopedia essay on Indian physics. I had written many prior essays on the subject, but unlike previous articles where I had gathered well-trodden material, I decided to focus on the 2,500 year old Vaiśeṣika Sūtra of Kaṇāda, which is the first systematic account of Indian physics. I was also attracted to this task as I had earlier translated the Yoga Sūtra and composed the Prajñā Sūtra (more of which will come later), and this would complete my sutra trilogy.

A formal scientific text in India is called *śāstra*, which is obtained using the instrument (*śastra*) of logic, and the convention is to write the śāstra in the pithy sutra form. The Vaiśeṣika Sūtra (VS) is a central Indian text, but somehow it was ignored by scholars during the past century or so. I have seen books mention that Kaṇāda presented an atomic theory of matter independent and prior to the atomic doctrine of Democritus and leave it at that.

As I began to study the VS I was astonished by the sophistication of the system. Concluding that Kaṇāda's work is a masterpiece of world science, I decided to spend all the time I could get to do a new translation along with a commentary.

The VS takes the world to be atomic, with atoms of four kinds. Each material substance is composed of these atoms, two (or perhaps three) of which have mass and the remaining do not. The ordinary molecules of matter have all the four basic atoms present in them for by heating a solid substance changes into liquid, and later into gas; with still further heating it burns, converting into heat and light.

The intuition behind the theory is that one atom is indicative of solidity and this is the heaviest; the second atom makes the liquid state possible and therefore it should be lighter; the third atom represents decay and it has (probably) no mass (this is not expressly stated); and the fourth is the constituent of light and heat and it definitely has no mass. It is astonishing that these atoms have turned out to be similar to proton, electron, neutrino, and photon.

The VS anticipates most of Newton's laws of motion, including the one on how an object continues in its state of rest or motion unless impressed with forces and that each action has an equal and opposite reaction.

The VS considers reality to have two aspects: physical and consciousness, with the two interacting when an observation is made. It anticipates the principle of psychophysical parallelism that lies at the basis of the Copenhagen Interpretation of quantum theory.

The Vaiśeṣika system has categories not only for space-time-matter but also for attributes related to perception of matter. It starts with six categories (padārthas) that are nameable and knowable, asserting that nothing beyond these six is necessary.

The six categories are: dravya (substance), guṇa (quality), karma (motion), sāmānya (universal), viśeṣa (particularity), and samavāya (inherence). The first three of these have objective existence and the last three are a product of intellectual discrimination. Universals (sāmānya) are recurrent generic properties in substances, qualities, and motions. Particularities (viśeṣa) reside exclusively in the eternal, non-composite substances, that is, in the individual atoms, souls, and minds, and in the unitary substances ether, space, and time. Inheritance (samavāya) is the relationship between entities that exist at the same time. It is the binding amongst categories that makes it possible to synthesize experience.

Of the six categories, the basic one is that of substance and the other five are qualities associated with the substance. Observers belong to the system in an integral fashion for if there were no sentient beings there would be no need for these categories.

There are nine classes of substances (dravya), some of which are non-atomic, some atomic, and others all-pervasive. The non-atomic ground is provided by the three substances of ether (ākāśa), space (dik), and time (kāla), which are unitary and indestructible; earth (pṛthvī), water (āpas), fire (tejas), and air (vāyu) are atomic composed of indivisible, and indestructible atoms (aṇu); self (ātman), which is the eighth, is omnipresent and eternal; and, lastly, the ninth, is the mind (manas), which is also eternal but of atomic dimensions, that is, infinitely small.

We could represent the basic atoms of pṛthvī, āpas, tejas, and vāyu by P, Ap, T, and V, respectively. The sequence of evolution of the elements in the Mahābhārata is given as V→T→Ap→P. Air is generally mentioned as the medium for the transmission of sound, but a more subtle sound that pervades the universe requires the more abstract vāyu. Four different forces govern the interactions of the atoms: P interacts with all the four, Ap with 3, T with 2, and V with 1.

Put simply, the main insight of the Vaiśeṣika is that consciousness is not to be found as a property that emerges out of matter. The best analogy to understand it is to take reality as a coin of which one side is physical matter and the other side is consciousness, and ordinarily neither may be reduced to the other. Kaṇāda says that consciousness cannot be a substance for it is not something that is modified by time or space, and therefore it should be a separate ontological category.

Kaṇāda speaks of *nitya* as a property that does not change or is invariant. From the perspective of physics, the idea of *nitya* is astonishingly modern. The property of *nitya* guarantees that the atom is spherical since it cannot have different characteristics along different directions.

While preparing my book on the VS, I tried to figure out why modern India has not made scientific contributions commensurate with its population. Is it because Indians are disconnected with their own scientific tradition or is it due to the pervasive culture of mediocrity that reigns in the higher education bureaucracy?

There were scientific giants in India before Independence and the names of Jagadish Chandra Bose, Satyendra Nath Bose, Meghnad Saha, C.V. Raman, Srinivasa Ramanujan and Yellapragada Subbarow come to mind. They made their contributions when there were few opportunities for research.

Compared to that difficult period, Indian universities were well supported after Independence. A few scientists have achieved greatness but they did so after leaving India. In any event, the contributions of Indian science since Independence are nowhere commensurate with the investment in higher education and the expansion of the university system.

In the West many scientists are interested in the philosophical basis of their research. They write on their experience for the general public and doing so bring the excitement of science to a wider audience. Few Indian scientists have written for the general public and, as far as I know, only J.C. Bose and C.V. Raman tried to present the philosophy underlying their research.

The second member of the sutra trilogy is the Yoga Sūtra of Patañjali that has, in recent years, become widely known for its subtle insights in the nature of the mind. It also serves as an advanced text for the worldwide yoga movement.

My interest in the Yoga Sūtra goes back to my college years but my formal translation came just a few years ago. Called *Mind and Self*, it has an introductory essay that examins its propositions from a scientific angle. I wanted the commentary to be informed by the newest ideas in science and place it within the larger context of Vedic wisdom, by separating the literal from the metaphorical. The special powers described in the Yoga Sūtra are insights that can help one master the outside world but do it in a manner that is consistent with science.

Yoga is not just about esoteric and other-worldly things; it is to prepare oneself for living life as fully as possible. Patañjali's propositions are based squarely on the Vedic idea of two selves, one the detached witness and the other the conditioned individual. This is described in the famous image of two birds on the tree (the body) of whom one is merely looking on whereas the other is eating the sweet fruit. The bird absorbed in sensory gratification is part of a causal chain, and not free; the one who is looking on is the universal witness.

Our capacity to obtain knowledge arises from freedom, and ignorance is the result of the coverings of habit that make us behave mechanically. The self is the lamp that shines light on the pool of the mind, but this light is ordinarlity scattered in so many different ways by ripples, distorting the image. The purpose of yogic practice is to make the pool of the mind clear so that one can reach one's true self and become creative.

A sister discipline to the Yoga is the Sāṅkhya, that deals with the interplay between consciousness (puruṣa) and matter (prakṛti). Matter has attributes (guṇas) of sattva (transparence), rajas (activity), and tamas (inactivity). Prakṛti is inert when the three guṇas are in a state of equilibrium but when it comes into contact with puruṣa, the balance of the guṇas is destroyed, which causes life to be created. The first to emerge from prakṛti is mahat, the cosmic intelligence, and buddhi, the intelligence of the individual. Out of mahat, the next lower category, ego (ahaṅkāra), is born; and out of the ego are born the individual mind (manas) and various organs of perception and action. These senses exist in subtle form as the tanmātras.

The evolution of Sāṅkhya is somewhat like modern evolution but also different in that it presupposes cosmic intelligence. Modern evolution implicitly uses intelligence when it speaks of optimization of function by Nature in its drive to select certain forms over others and abstractions such as beauty are universals. In modern science, consciousness is an emergent local property whereas in the Sāṅkhya it is an all-pervading category.

For consciousness to be incorporated into psychology or physics, process signatures of the tanmātras or something akin to it will have to be found.

———

The third sutra of the trilogy is the one that I came by on a flight from Washington, DC, to Houston in 2003. I scribbled the 18 statements of it on a page torn from the airline magazine and later wrote a commentary. Published as *The Prajñā Sūtra: Aphorisms of Intuition*, this sutra presents the Vedic understanding in terms of the triad of

221

interconnectedness (*bandhu*), paradox (*parokṣa*), and transcendence (*yajña*).

The interconnectedness of the perceived world arises from its unity and it is expressed across categories and scale. It is the source of recursion that forms an element of sacred geometry that was described earlier in the chapter on Vedic astronomy.

Recursion is seen in physical structures in nature and in social networks and biology, as in the example of animal societies. One of the hallmarks of recursion is scale invariance, which is confirmed by traffic and economic networks.

The ants in an ant colony may be compared to cells, their castes to tissues and organs, the queen and her drones to the generative system, and the exchange of liquid food amongst the colony members to the circulation of blood and lymph. Furthermore, corresponding to morphogenesis in organisms the ant colony has sociogenesis, which consists of the processes by which the individuals undergo changes in caste and behavior.

The queen produces the workers of the correct size for her initial survival and later, after the colony has started going, she produces a complement of workers of different sizes as well as soldier ants in order to have the right organization for the survival of the colony. When members of a specific caste from an ongoing colony are removed, the queen compensates for this deficit by producing more members of that caste.

In its embodiment, the unity of reality is replaced by duality, not only in the separation of the subject and the object, but also the separation between one object and another. Boundaries imply interaction, and within each system one can likewise see boundaries repeated in smaller parts. Within the heart of the individual there are two tendencies: one related to unity, and the other to separation. The churning of the ocean is not only mythic history; it is also the story of each individual's life. It tells us that the asuras (the embodiment of objectification) and the devas (the embodiment of unity) reside within each individual.

Paradoxes are inevitable due to the fact that language cannot capture all aspects of the duality of the embodied reality. Each theory has limitations of applicability revealing paradox when examined at the fringes of this domain. Therefore, both ideology and models of science are limited. By pushing science to limits we arrive at new puzzles, motivating us to to create new models that help uncover hidden layers of reality.

Transcendence is associated with insight and development. In Sanskrit the word yajña, usually translated as sacrifice, is sometimes used for it. Unless we are machines, we must transcend the previous self to become a new person and in that sense the process is a sacrifice.

26. Looking Ahead

Ideas have consequences. The wrong but fashionable idea that all nations desire Western-style democracy was a motivation for the disastrous American invasion of Iraq. This was compounded by the subsequent Western support for uprisings against Arab dictators that begat ISIS and its untold attendant horrors. Prior to this, in the 60s and 70s, Americans unleashed war on Vietnam due to their misreading of Vietnamese culture.

The erroneous idea that all cultures see the world the same way is preventing Europe from finding a solution to the problem of refugees. To interact creatively with another culture requires understanding of the other, but the West insists on using its categories, refusing to engage with the migrants on their own terms.

The West has pretensions that its refinements are universal, and no doubt American pop culture holds the world in thrall. In truth, it is one window on reality which is based on a materialistic approach to life.

The post-industrial West rejects traditional practices and beliefs and accepts individual freedoms unfettered by social custom. Those who wish to destroy the West hate these freedom as well as the West's values, art, and mores, although they may love its comforts.

Interaction between cultures without mutual understanding leads to disaster. The Aztecs and the Inca did not know the categories of the Spaniards whereas the Spaniards had a good sense of their enemy. This asymmetry of knowledge made it possible for Hernan Cortes and just a few hundred soldiers to defeat the Aztecs in 1521, and twelve years later Francisco Pizarro with a similarly small group conquered the Inca Empire.

There is no absolute reality that is wholly a product of nature. A culture is like a lens through which people construct their world. This happens both with the vocabulary of the language of the culture as well myths, rituals, manners, and history. If a specific concept has no word in a language then that concept is unlikely to play an important role in the politics and social customs of that culture.

The arts are a good place to see the deep influence of the collective mind. Nature is an important subject in Chinese and Japanese art, and landscape painting is especially valued.

The Japanese haiku uses the simplest happenings in nature to communicate deep felt experience and insight as in these famous haiku (17-syllable poem) by Basho (1644-1694):

an ancient pond / a frog jumps in / the splash of water

now then, let's go out / to enjoy the snow... until / I slip and fall!

The Indian arts are based on Purāṇic themes with abstractions removed from ordinary lived life, and much Indian poetry is mystical and religious. When the Turks ruled India, the disenfranchised elite retreated into Tantra, esoteric philosophy, and epic poetry.

The educated Chinese, who were barred from high government jobs during the Mongol Yuan dynasty, had literary gatherings in their estates that were commemorated in natural paintings with the code that the prosperous house will be represented by a thatched hut.

Language and culture affect how we perceive and create our world. The simplest example of this is the experience of color. There are languages in which there are no separate words for green and blue, and the same word refers to either of the two, based on the context.

William Gladstone, who was the prime minister of Great Britain four separate times in the 19th Century, was a classicist who wrote a book on Homeric language. He noted that Homeric poetry hardly ever used the word for blue, using porphyreos, "purple" or "dark red," to describe blood, a dark cloud, a wave, and a rainbow, and oinops ("wine-looking") when speaking of the sea. Gladstone suggested that the ancient Greeks used colors mainly in terms of light/dark contrasts, rather than in terms of hue.

Sanskrit has similar ambiguity, but between green and yellow-golden. The principal words used for green are harit, palāśa, śyāmavarṇa, whereas those for yellow-golden are hari, hiraṇya, pīta, gauraḥ, haridrābhāḥ. The same word hari represents both green and yellow (golden), and hari for golden in Sanskrit is like zari in Persian.

All this doesn't mean that the ancients were either deficient in their usage of words or colorblind. The convention for the use of adjectives was different. Plants (and other objects) were associated with one color-name, which is green initially but changes to yellow when ripe.

The transition from the complexity of meaning in the ancient world to a more definite one is one hallmark of modern times. This transition parallels an emphasis away from contextual definition to one that is stand-alone. If in the ancient world one derived comfort and happiness in family and community, in the modern one must find these in oneself.

The idea of sensate pleasure has to a large degree replaced happiness. But these pleasures often come with loneliness, which is made worse in the age of the Internet where personal social interactions have lessened.

The migrant upon leaving traditional society and entering the West is soon dismayed by the isolation of the lived life. While he sees that the individual has freedom and possessions indicate success, he is frustrated by the complex web of rules that must be negotiated to move ahead.

It is not that only the migrant is disoriented. The unprecedented changes in society have also created dislocation in old communities which explains the current meth, heroin, and painkiller medicine epidemic sweeping the West. Some argue that the demeaning of the West's own spiritual tradition by the elites has exacerbated the problem. Others argue that dealing with the uncertainty of modern life is a connection with one's own true self, which explains the ever-growing popularity of yoga.

Not knowing the way to relate to a world that looks orderly and beautiful on the surface but is frightening deeper down, it is easy for many to be swept off the feet by heroic stories of conquest and martyrdom.

———

As we look at the past and the possible futures from our present perch in time, we see a period of deep uncertainty. Although, technologies of the past few centuries changed society by extending our senses in the capacity to travel, communicate, see and hear, they have alienated us from our nature. Newer artificial intelligence technologies have within them the additional danger that they will displace humansin most jobs.

After the Industrial Revolution, tasks that required human and animal labor were increasingly turned over to machines, first in richer nations and then elsewhere. In my own childhood in small villages of Kashmir there were no machines. My mother used firewood in an open mud stove for cooking and in some villages there was no electricity, piped water, or telephone. The only thing that made our life different from that of our forebears was the bus that took us from one place to another.

The invention of the sewing machines, steam power, and iron mills took the drudgery out of tasks that had been done manually for thousands of years. One of the most important inventions was the cotton gin for the separation of cotton balls from the seeds. Although a painting in Ajanta (fifth century) appears to show a single roller gin that later gave way to double rollers, the modern cotton gin machine was invented by Eli Whitney in the United States in 1793. Made of wood, the machine used metal hooks attached on the side of panels to remove the seeds. With this machine the efficiency of the seed separation process increased fifty-fold.

This invention had the unintended consequence of growth of slavery. As cotton farming became extremely profitable, the demand for land and slave labor increased. Before the invention there were six slave states; by 1846, there were fifteen. Historians believe that this machine was one of the indirect causes of the American Civil War.

The march of industrialization has accelerated and its current evolution is qualitatively different from the previous phases. Newest machines can do jobs where traditionally human intelligence was needed. We are entering the age of intelligent machines. As economies adjust, new jobs being created are either too specialized, where not many workers are needed, or low-paying jobs in the service sector.

Experimental self-driven cars are already on the road. Agriculture and animal husbandry have become industrialized in the developed nations, and robots are replacing workers at the assembly line. As the share of manufacturing and production in the economy becomes progressively smaller at the expense of services and entertainment, even the education sector is being affected. With China becoming the world's manufacturing hub, many traditional crafts have disappeared, and even the images used in Indian temples are imported.

Countries are adjusting to the loss of jobs by emphasizing tourism, crafts, and infrastructure development. Conservative societies with cultural biases against tourism are finding this adjustment difficult which is particularly true of countries in northern Africa and the Middle East. Their unprecedented unemployment is a driver for migration to Europe, America, and Australia.

Middle class jobs in developed countries have also disappeared but these economies have responded by instituting generous unemployment benefits, which serve as a pull for the migrants.

Another factor in the mix is the demographic collapse in the developed world. The German population is expected to fall by twenty percent by 2060 in spite of continuing immigration, and by that time many small towns across the country will be depopulated. Likewise, Portugal's population is expected to drop by thirty percent.

European nations are admitting millions of migrants to mitigate their own population decline. But this comes with a big unknown for the future since the immigrants do not wish to assimilate.

The emergence of Islamic State as the new Caliphate has complicated the picture further. A consequence of the destabilization of the region by the Iraq War and the unresolved schisms within Islam, it has tremendous hold on the imagination of the disaffected Muslim youth worldwide. Islamic law supports death penalty for apostasy and until this is changed, there will be one group or another that will call out those who disagree as apostates who deserves death. Indeed, this is how the Sunnis and the Shias characterize each other.

It is inevitable that the conflict between Islamist ideology and the West will go on for years and societies will adjust to random acts of terror. The danger is for violence to get out of hand in response to acts of provocation. True believers want an all-out war in the hope that passion and religious faith will bring them victory.

The welfare state of the West cannot last forever; indeed, most of the European nations are bankrupt. When the welfare benefits to the unemployed end, new challenges will threaten social harmony.

History repeats itself, but each time with a twist. Behind Rome's decline was a similar mix of the desire for efficiency, immigration and unemployment. In late Roman Empire big farms, called latifundia, used the best technology of the day to cut the cost of production. Slaves from far-flung colonies of the Empire were brought in to work on the estates, which were consolidated into ever-larger size.

As more slaves came in, wages became depressed and unemployment among the citizens increased. Rome responded by instituting the dole, consisting of pork, oil and bread, for the unemployed and subsidies to farmers. With time, the Empire's finances became overstretched and the army became dependent on foreign recruits and mercenaries. Inflation increased, the provinces rose in revolt, and, as always, barbarians were knocking at the gate. It was in this vacuum that religion stepped in and took Europe into the Dark Ages.

Recent developments in Europe and the US in response to the pressures of globalization parallel those of Late Rome. Like the owners of the latifundia, the tech titans want ever-larger immigration quotas for programmers to keep the wages down.

Will the world go the way of the dark vision of Aldous Huxley in his *Brave New World*? Huxley saw the Alphas, with the assistance of the Betas, running the World State, with the menial tasks left to the Gammas, the Deltas, and the Epsilons, who were dulled by drugs and recreational sex. He saw a general mockery of marriage, parenthood, and pregnancy.

Indian social theorists, in the dharmaśāstras, foresaw the problem of disparity which is why they exalted the idea of renunciation. To them the pursuit of happiness was a subtle dance between enjoyment and sacrifice.

Social fabric will be severely strained as fewer and fewer people are needed to work farms and factories. It is fear of this future, and pressures of work if they hold a job and despair if they are unemployed, that is influencing more and more people not to have children.

Virtual reality, drugs, movies and TV shows and social media provide pursuits that can keep a person busy the entire day. Individualism has degenerated into Narcissism and the cult of the body.

Information is central to modern business and politics. The media, as arbiter of what is good information, has allied itself with powerful political and corporate groups. In a networked society, the state needs increased control over the lives of people and propaganda is a tool used for the control. Technology has facilitated the centralization of power. Once a stable state has been arrived at, individuals do not have much freedom to go against the "consensus."

———

As populations decrease in Europe and America, both the left and the right are clamoring for greater immigration: The left, for it will reduce the political power of entrenched groups, even though it depresses wages; the right, for cheap labor.

With the march of technology many are convinced that somehow we are also machines, and life has no real meaning except for the pleasures of the senses and exercise of power. Many countries that gained political freedom in recent past have slipped into dictatorships and rule by religious zealots.

New technologies are a double-edged sword. While some media makes it easier to exercise control, alternate media has reduced the power of the establishment. But if social media can bring the sense of freedom, it can also bind people into delusional cults.

Seventy years after the end of the Second World War, the consensus that led to scientific and economic progress has lost its hold on many people. We like it that machines are taking on more of our tedious tasks, but where will this stop, if at all? Will the future be a world with real freedom for just a few at the very top of the pyramid, with the rest encouraged to live in imagined spaces aided by virtual reality and addictions of different kinds? Or will mankind choose a new path of wisdom and compassion that makes it possible for all to achieve their creative potential? This latter path will require an understanding of the mystery of consciousness.